ISO 9001:2000
Explained

Also Available from ASQ Quality Press

ISO 9000 at the Front Line
William A. Levinson, Roger Bishop, Barbara Heffron, and Martin Wentz

Internal Quality Auditing
Denis Pronovost

ISO Lesson Guide: The Pocket Guide to Q9001:2000
J.P. Russell and Dennis Arter

ISO 9000 Implementation for Small Business
James L. Lamprecht

Eight-Step Process to Successful ISO 9000 Implementation: A Quality Management System Approach
Lawrence A. Wilson

The Quality Audit Handbook, Second Edition
ASQ Quality Audit Division, J.P. Russell Editing Director

ISO 9000 Quality Management System Design: Optimal Design Rules for Documentation, Implementation, and System Effectiveness
Jay J. Schlickman

ISO 9000: A Legal Perspective
Dr. James W. Kolka

After the Quality Audit: Closing the Loop on the Audit Process,
Second Edition
J.P. Russell and Terry L. Regel

Aviation Industry Quality Systems: ISO 9000 and the Federal Aviation Regulations
Michael J. Dreikorn

Meet the Registrar: Firsthand Accounts of ISO 9000 Success from the Registration Source
C. Michael Taylor

To request a complimentary copy of ASQ Quality Press publications, call 800-248-1946, or visit our online bookstore at http://qualitypress.asq.org .

ISO 9001:2000
Explained

Charles A. Cianfrani
Joseph J. Tsiakals
Jack West

ASQ Quality Press
Milwaukee, Wisconsin

ISO 9001:2000 Explained
Charles A. Cianfrani, Joseph J. Tsiakals, Jack West

Library of Congress Cataloging-in-Publication Data

Tsiakals, Joseph J.
　　ISO 9001:2000 explained / Joseph J. Tsiakals, Charles A. Cianfrani, Jack West.
　　　p. cm.
　　ISBN 0-87389-481-2 (alk. paper)
　　　1. ISO 9000 Series Standards. I. Cianfrani, Charles A. II. West, Jack, 1944-

　　TS156.6. T78 2000
　　658.5'62—dc21   00-025278

© 2000 by ASQ

10 9 8 7 6 5 4 3 2

ISBN 0-87389-481-2

Acquisitions Editor: Ken Zielske
Project Editor: Annemieke Koudstaal
Production Administrator: Shawn Dohogne
Special Marketing Representative: Matthew Meinholz

ASQ Mission: The American Society for Quality advances individual and organizational performance excellence worldwide by providing opportunities for learning, quality improvement, and knowledge exchange.

Attention: Bookstores, Wholesalers, Schools and Corporations:
ASQ Quality Press books, videotapes, audiotapes, and software are available at quantity discounts with bulk purchases for business, educational, or instructional use. For information, please contact ASQ Quality Press at 800-248-1946, or write to ASQ Quality Press, P.O. Box 3005, Milwaukee, WI 53201-3005.

To place orders or to request a free copy of the ASQ Quality Press Publications Catalog, including ASQ membership information, call 800-248-1946. Visit our web site at www.asq.org .

Printed in the United States of America

∞ Printed on acid-free paper

American Society for Quality

ASQ

Quality Press
611 East Wisconsin Avenue
Milwaukee, Wisconsin 53202
Call toll free 800-248-1946
www.asq.org
http://qualitypress.asq.org
http://standardsgroup.asq.org

Contents

Preface

The ISO 9000 family of quality standards was initially issued in 1987, and minor revision was issued in 1994. Over the past several years, the ISO technical committee responsible for this family has undertaken a major project to update the standards and to make the documents more user-friendly. ISO 9001:2000 represents the first major revision to the standard since its initial issue. Some of the major changes include the following:

- Use of a process approach and a new structure for the standard that is built around a process model that considers all work in terms of inputs and outputs
- Shift in emphasis from documenting the system in procedures to a focus on developing and managing a family of effective processes
- Greater emphasis on the role of top management
- More emphasis on the customer, including understanding needs, meeting requirements, and measuring customer satisfaction/dissatisfaction
- Emphasis on setting measurable objectives and on measuring product and process performance
- Introduction of requirements for analysis and use of data to define opportunities for improvement
- Formalization of the concept of continual improvement of the quality management system
- Use of wording that is more easily understood in all product sectors—not just hardware
- Provision for *permissible exclusions* in ISO 9001:2000, which facilitates elimination of ISO 9002 and ISO 9003

This book addresses the needs of the following:

- Organizations seeking a general understanding of the contents of ISO 9001:2000
- Organizations desiring guidance to facilitate migration of an ISO 9001:1994–compliant quality management system to become compliant with ISO 9001:2000
- Organizations considering the use of ISO 9001:2000 as a foundation for the development of a comprehensive quality management system

This book explains the meaning and intent of the requirements of ISO/DIS 9001:2000 (the Draft International Standard issued in November, 1999) and discusses the requirements as they relate to each of the product categories. Where appropriate, it includes an elaboration of why the requirements are important. Key changes from the 1994 standard are identified. Finally, it includes a list of typical audit-type questions that an organization may consider to appraise compliance with the requirements.

Symbols are used to designate the following:

 Identifies changes or new requirements from ISO 9001:1994

 Provides definitions from ISO/DIS 9000:2000

 Lists typical audit items to appraise compliance with the requirements of ISO/DIS 9001:2000

 Describes considerations for documentation

This book contains the text of ISO/DIS 9001:2000 (November 25, 1999) as contained in the proposed US adoption of this standard (BSR/ISO/ASQ Q9001-2000). It also provides the ISO/DIS 9000:2000 definitions of key words as contained in the proposed US adoption of this standard (BSR/ISO/ASQ Q9000-2000).

CHAPTER
1

Introduction

0 Introduction

0.1 General

This International Standard specifies requirements for a quality management system that can be used by an organization to address customer satisfaction, by meeting customer and applicable regulatory requirements. It can also be used by internal and external parties, including certification bodies, to assess the organization's ability to meet customer and regulatory requirements.

The adoption of a quality management system needs to be a strategic decision of the organization. The design and implementation of an organization's quality management system is influenced by varying needs, particular objectives, the products provided, the processes employed and the size and structure of the organization. It is not the purpose of this International Standard to imply uniformity in the structure of quality management systems or uniformity of documentation.

It is emphasized that the quality management system requirements specified in this International Standard are complementary to technical requirements for products.

Source: BSR/ISO/ASQ Q9001-2000.

The introductory material in clause 0 and its subclauses is called "informative" in ISO language meaning that it does not form part of the requirements of ISO 9001:2000. It exists to provide context, general understanding, and background.

This subclause discusses the intent of ISO 9001, the flexibility of the standard and why organizations should use it. This can be summarized as follows:

- Figure 1 represents *one model* that can be used to describe how the process approach may be applied to quality management systems. There is no implication that Figure 1 is the ideal model or that it is the only model that can be used.

0.3 Relationship with ISO 9004

This edition of ISO 9001 has been developed as one part of a consistent pair of quality management system standards, the other being ISO 9004:2000. The two International Standards are designed to be used together, but can also be used independently. Although the two International Standards have different scopes, they have similar structures for ease of use.

This edition of ISO 9001 specifies requirements for a quality management system that may be used for internal application by organizations, certification, or contractual purposes.

ISO 9004:2000 gives guidance on a wider range of objectives of a quality management system to improve an organization's overall performance. ISO 9004:2000 is not a guideline for implementing ISO 9001:2000 and is not intended for certification or contractual use.

Source: BSR/ISO/ASQ Q9001-2000.

Clause 0.3 describes the relationship between the ISO/DIS 9001:2000 requirements document and ISO/DIS 9004:2000, which provides guidelines for a quality management system that is focused on performance improvement. Often identified as a "consistent pair" of quality management system standards, these two documents can be compared as follows:

- The two standards have very different scopes. ISO/DIS 9004 is not intended for certification or contractual use, and it is not intended to provide guidance for implementing ISO/DIS 9001:2000. ISO/DIS 9004:2000 also is not intended to be used as a basis for audit of the quality management system.

- ISO/DIS 9004:2000 does provide guidance that can be used to improve the overall performance of the organization. To facilitate its use for improvement, its structure is consistent with that of ISO/DIS 9001:2000.

0.4 Compatibility with other management systems

This International Standard is intended to be compatible with other internationally recognized management system standards. It is aligned with ISO 14001:1996 in order to enhance the compatibility of the two standards for the benefit of the user community.

This International Standard does not include requirements specific to other management systems, such as those particular to environmental management, occupational health and safety management, or financial management. However, this International Standard allows an organization to align or integrate its own quality management system with related management system requirements. In some cases, it may be possible for an organization to adapt its existing management system(s) in order to establish a quality management system that complies with the requirements of this International Standard.

Source: BSR/ISO/ASQ Q9001-2000.

Clause 0.4, *Compatibility with other management systems,* states that the standard has been developed with specific intent to be compatible with the ISO 14001:1996 *Environmental management systems—Specification with guidance for use.* In the opinion of most experts, there has always been good compatibility between ISO 14001:1996 and ISO 9001:1994. The drafters of the two families have worked together during the development of ISO/DIS 9001:2000 to ensure this compatibility is maintained. In fact, experts from ISO TC 210, the technical committee responsible for ISO 14001, were participants in the working group that drafted ISO/DIS 9001:2000.

Considerations related to compatibility include the following:

- ISO/DIS 9001:2000 was structured to enhance its usability with ISO 14001.
- ISO/DIS 9001:2000 and ISO 14001:1996 can be used together without unnecessary duplication or conflicting requirements.
- Common requirements can form a basis for integrated management systems.
- Quality management system processes need not be established separate from an existing management system.

1 Scope

1.1 General

This International Standard specifies requirements for a quality management system where an organization needs

a) to demonstrate its ability to provide consistently product that meets customer and applicable regulatory requirements, and

b) to address customer satisfaction through the effective application of the system, including processes for continual improvement and the prevention of nonconformity.

NOTE Monitoring of customer satisfaction, as stated in b), requires the evaluation of information relating to customer perceptions of whether or not the organization has met the customer requirements.

The requirements specified in this International Standard are generic and applicable to all organizations, regardless of type, size and product provided.

It is intended that all requirements of this International Standard be applied. However, certain requirements may be excluded in particular situations (see 1.2).

Source: BSR/ISO/ASQ Q9001-2000.

Earlier it was indicated that clause 0 and its subclauses are "informative" and do not form part of the requirements of ISO/DIS 9001:2000. The scope is a normative part of the standard, but the ISO directives also specify that the topics in clause 1 also must not contain requirements. Part 3 of the ISO directives states that the scope of a standard ". . . shall be succinct so that it can be used as a summary for bibliographic purposes. This element shall be worded as a series of statements of fact." Clause 1 therefore does not use the word *shall,* the keyword in ISO standards that makes a statement a requirement. As summarized in the following list, the scope contains material that describes how the standard is used.

- The intent is that ISO/DIS 9001:2000 be directly usable by all types and sizes of organizations regardless of product category.
- The scope makes it clear that an ISO/DIS 9001:2000 compliant quality management system is aimed at achieving customer satisfaction by meeting requirements.

ISO/DIS 9001:2000 is comprehensive in that it applies to all quality management system processes from identification of requirements to delivery and addressing of customer satisfaction.

The scope also contains a significant note. This note states that monitoring of customer satisfaction requires evaluation of information on customers' *perceptions* of whether the organization has met requirements. In ISO standards, a note is not a requirement and thus is not auditable. The note in this clause does provide a strong bias regarding the robustness of the quality management system processes that should be considered when an organization addresses the requirement to measure customer satisfaction and/or dissatisfaction.

1.2 Permissible exclusions

The organization may only exclude quality management system requirements that neither affect the organization's ability, nor absolve it from its responsibility, to provide product that meets customer and applicable regulatory requirements. These exclusions are limited to those requirements within clause 7 (see also 5.5.5), and may be due to the following:

a) the nature of the organization's product;

b) customer requirements;

c) the applicable regulatory requirements.

Where permissible exclusions are exceeded, conformity to this International Standard should not be claimed. This includes situations where the fulfilment of regulatory requirements permits exclusions that exceed those allowed by this International Standard.

Source: BSR/ISO/ASQ Q9001-2000.

The 1994 edition of the ISO 9000 family includes three requirement standards and a number of guidance documents. The 1994 requirement standards were as follows:

- ISO 9001, *Quality systems—Model for quality assurance in design/development, production, installation, and servicing*
- ISO 9002, *Quality systems—Model for quality assurance in production, installation, and servicing*
- ISO 9003, *Quality systems—Model for quality assurance in final inspection and test*

This arrangement provided a structure in which an organization could use the minimal ISO 9003 if it were appropri-

ate to control only the detection and correction of nonconforming product. ISO 9002:1994 was intended for application
by organizations where design and/or development were
not performed by the organization.

ISO 9001:1994 was to be used when all aspects of
design, production, installation, and servicing are applicable.

The new ISO/DIS 9001:2000 revision eliminates the ISO
9002 and 9003 documents. The permissible-exclusions clause
provides instructions on how to accommodate the elimination
of ISO 9002 and ISO 9003. Key points of the permissible-
exclusions clause include the following:

- An organization can exclude requirements within clause 7
  that are not required by a customer or by the nature of the
  product and/or service provided.

- An organization cannot exclude requirements that affect
  ability to provide conforming product and/or service.

Organizations have excluded activities covered by the
1994 editions when those activities were not performed
and had no affect on conformity with customer requirements. Organizations typically use the quality manual to
designate the specific requirements that are not included.
The new permissible-exclusions clause only recognizes this
reality.

On the other hand, many organizations that perform
product design activities have used ANSI/ISO/ASQC Q9002-
1994, which excludes design. With the new standard, this will
not be acceptable. Organizations that perform design work
and desire to achieve compliance with ISO/DIS 9001:2000
must address design requirements in their quality management systems based on ISO/DIS 9001:2000. The permissible
exclusions must be defined in the quality manual but do not
absolve the organization of the responsibility to meet customer requirements.

Organizations need to exercise great care in excluding
activities from their system. The clause clearly states that
an organization may not claim compliance with ISO/DIS
9001:2000 if quality management system exclusions exceed
what is permitted in clause 1.2.

A second important aspect of the permissible-exclusions clause is the relationship of ISO/DIS 9001:2000 to regulatory requirements. Regulations absolutely take precedence. This issue is critical to many users of the standard. Therefore, ISO/DIS 9001:2000 has been carefully developed to be able to be used to address regulatory needs. Today, ISO 9001:1994 is indicated in certain regulations as one approach for meeting the regulatory requirements for the design and production of various products. The intent of the permissible exclusions clause is to facilitate continued use of ISO/DIS 9001: 2000 by organizations that are required to address regulatory requirements.

When scope is reduced, regulatory requirements are still applicable. If scope is reduced further than permitted by the standard, the system is not ISO/DIS 9001:2000 compliant.

---

2 Normative reference

The following normative document contains provisions which, through reference in this text, consitute provisions of this International Standard. For dated references, subsequent amendments to, or revisions of, this publication do not apply. However, parties to agreements based on this International Standard are encouraged to investigate the possibility of applying the most recent edition of the normative document indicated below. Members of ISO and IEC maintain registers of currently valid International Standards.

ISO 9000:2000, *Quality management systems— Fundamentals and vocabulary*

Source: BSR/ISO/ASQ Q9001-2000.

3 Terms and definitions

For the purposes of this International Standard, the terms and definitions given in ISO 9000:2000, and the following, apply.

NOTE The terms used in this edition of this International Standard to describe the supply-chain are as follows:

supplier ⟶ organization ⟶ customer

The term "organization" replaces the previously used term "supplier", to mean the unit to which this International Standard applies. Ther term "supplier" is now used instead of the previous term "subcontractor". The changes have been introduced to reflect the vocabulary used by organizations.

3.1 product

result of a process

NOTE 1 There are four agreed generic product categories:
—hardware,
—software,
—services,
—processed materials.

Most products are combinations of some of the four generic product categories. Whether the combined product is then called hardware, processed material, software or service depends on the dominant element.

NOTE 2 Adapted from ISO 9000:2000.

Source: BSR/ISO/ASQ Q9001-2000.

The only normative reference in ISO/DIS 9001:2000 is ISO/DIS 9000:2000, which contains the terms and definitions used in the ISO 9000 family. The only normative content of ISO/DIS 9000:2000 is the actual definitions. Key points from clauses 2 and 3 include the following:

- ISO 9000:2000 contains definitions that are normative and form part of the requirements.

- Supply-chain terminology is used to be consistent with language that is commonly used in the ordinary course of operations:

   Supplier ⎯⎯⎯➤ organization ⎯⎯⎯➤ customer

- The definition of the word *product* is included to emphasize that a product is any output from a process. This includes services as well as the other product categories that are listed. Inclusion of the definition emphasizes the general applicability of ISO 9001 to all types of products, including services.

CHAPTER

2

Quality Management System and General Documentation

4 Quality management system

4.1 General requirements

The organization shall establish, document, implement, maintain and continually improve a quality management system in accordance with the requirements of this International Standard.

To implement the quality management system, the organization shall:

a) identify the processes needed for the quality management system;

b) determine the sequence and interaction of these processes;

c) determine criteria and methods required to ensure the effective operation and control of these processes;

d) ensure the availability of information necessary to support the operation and monitoring of these processes;

e) measure, monitor and analyze these processes, and implement action necessary to achieve planned results and continual improvement.

The organization shall manage these processes in accordance with the requirements of this International Standard.

Source: BSR/ISO/ASQ Q9001-2000.

The basic requirement for a quality management system is that the organization must identify and manage the family of processes needed to ensure conformity. The quality management system ensures compliance with the quality policy and that quality objectives are met. Organizations should not lose sight of this basic concept. It is easy to get so absorbed in documenting a system that the basic concept is lost. While documentation is important, the primary emphasis should be on developing and implementing effective quality management system processes.

 It is critical to understand the difference between managing a system and documenting a system. Clause 4.1 does not directly address documentation. Rather, clause 4.1 requires that processes be developed and implemented to make up the overall system. It also requires that processes be managed and continually improved. These improvement activities must include measurement, monitoring, and analysis of the processes. This is at the heart of the *process approach* and represents one of the major changes in focus from ISO 9001:1994.

The activities that organizations will need to consider include the following:

- Identification of processes and their interrelationships, sequences, and interactions
- Establishment of criteria and means to effectively operate, control, measure, and analyze the processes
- Improvement of the quality management system, which includes improvement of these processes

Understanding and using this process approach is critical to compliance with ISO/DIS 9001:2000 because, as we will see in the next section, the requirements for documented procedures have been dramatically reduced.

 DEFINITIONS

Management system (2.2.2)—system to establish policy and objectives and to achieve those objectives

NOTE   A management system of an organization may include different management systems, such as a quality management system, a financial management system, or an environmental management system

Organization (2.3.1.)—group of people and facilities with an orderly arrangement of responsibilities, authorities, and relationships

EXAMPLES   Company, corporation, firm, enterprise, institution, charity, sole trader, association, or parts or combinations thereof.

NOTE 1   An organization can be incorporated, public or private.

NOTE 2   This definition is valid for the purposes of quality management systems standards. The term "organization" is defined differently in ISO/IEC Guide 2.

Process (2.4.1)—system of activities which uses resources to transform inputs into outputs

NOTE 1   Inputs to a process are typically outputs of other processes.

NOTE 2   Processes in an organization typically are planned and carried out under controlled conditions to add value.

NOTE 3   A process where the conformity of the resulting product cannot be readily or economically verified is frequently referred to as a "special process".

Quality (2.1.1)—ability of a set of inherent characteristics of a product, system or process to fulfil requirements of customers and other interested parties

NOTE   The term "quality" may be used with adjectives such as poor, good or excellent.

Quality management system (2.2.3)—system to establish a quality policy and quality objectives and to achieve those objectives

Requirement (2.1.2)—need or expectation that is stated, customarily implied or obligatory

NOTE 1   A qualifier may be used to denote a specific type of requirement, e.g. product requirement, quality system requirement, customer requirement.

NOTE 2   A specified requirement is one which is stated, for example, in a document.

NOTE 3   Requirements may be generated by different interested parties.

Source: BSR/ISO/ASQ Q9000-2000.

 # TYPICAL AUDIT ITEMS FOR COMPLIANCE

Items representing a difference from ISO 9001:1994 have a Δ at the end.

- Have the processes needed for quality management been identified? Δ

- Has sequence and interaction of these processes been determined? Δ
- Have criteria and control methods been determined for control of the processes in the quality management system? Δ
- Is information available to support operation and monitoring of the processes? Δ
- Are processes measured, monitored, and analyzed with appropriate actions taken to achieve planned results and continual improvement? Δ
- Is the quality management system established, documented, implemented, maintained, and continually improved? Δ

4.2 General documentation requirements

The quality management system documentation shall include:

a) documented procedures required in this International Standard;

b) documents required by the organization to ensure the effective operation and control of its processes.

NOTE 1 Where the term "documented procedure" appears within this International Standard, this requires the procedure to be established, documented, implemented and maintained.

The extent of the quality management system documentation shall be dependent on the following:

a) size and type of the organization;

b) complexity and interaction of the processes;

c) competence of personnel.

NOTE 2 The documented procedures and documents may be in any form or type of medium.

Source: BSR/ISO/ASQ Q9001-2000.

Documentation forms a basis for understanding the system, communicating its processes and requirements within the organization, describing it to other organizations, and determining the effectiveness of implementation. The organization is required to establish, document, maintain, and improve the quality management system. It is clearly management's responsibility to facilitate establishment of the system. Management must also ensure that the system is actually implemented; it is obviously insufficient to have a documented system that is not implemented. The documented system must reflect actual activities that are performed to ensure conformity.

On the other hand, the perceived requirement for an excessive number of documented procedures has been one of the most criticized aspects of ISO 9001:1994. ISO/DIS 9001:2000 makes a significant step toward changing that perception. The emphasis has shifted from documenting procedures that address twenty elements to managing a system of processes to achieve specific quality objectives. It is the process management described earlier that is important. Organizations have always had freedom to determine the extent of documentation that is appropriate. With ISO/DIS 9001:2000 they will now have even more flexibility to select documentation methods and structures that are appropriate for the organization's needs.

The system must also be maintained. Nothing is static; changes occur constantly in most organizations. This means the system must be used on an ongoing basis and must be kept current.

The extent of the quality management system documentation for an organization is dependent on the organization's situation. As a minimum, the documentation must include an appropriate combination of the following documents:

- The *quality manual* must describe the sequence and interaction of the processes in the quality management system. ISO/DIS 9001:2000 requires that the organization have a quality manual and that the manual meets certain specific requirements. The details of these requirements are given in clause 5.5.6 and will be discussed in chapter 3. The manual must either contain or reference the *documented procedures* that give greater detail of the system's processes.

- There must be *documented procedures* that describe the system. These procedures must either be included as a part of, or referenced in, the quality manual. ISO/DIS 9001:2000 specifically requires "documented procedures" in only six places, *but* remember that the organization must also have documentation of the system's processes and their interactions. Once the processes of the quality management system have been defined and their interactions established, the key processes should be described in documented procedures. Along with the quality manual, these documented procedures provide a mechanism for communication of the processes to the organization. As will be discussed in chapter 3, clause 5.5.4 requires communication of processes to the appropriate functions and levels of the organization. A well-prepared quality manual along with easily understood procedures is a means to address a key element of the internal communications requirement.

It may come as a surprise to many that ISO/DIS 9001:2000 has far fewer specific requirements for documented procedures than ISO 9001:1994. Table 2.1 illustrates the differences. It is important to remember that clause 4.2b requires the organization to identify and prepare any documents necessary for the effective operation of the quality management system. Organizations typically need additional documentation to fully describe the quality management system

- *Other system documentation* is required as necessary to document the sequences and activities required for the operation of the system. In addition to the quality manual and the documented procedures that describe the overall processes of the quality management system, organizations are specifically required to prepare other documentation needed for control of processes. The type and extent of these documents must be determined by the organization. This documentation is typically in the form of written procedures or work instructions. Table 2.2 provides a listing of the clauses in ISO/DIS 9001:2000 where such documentation is discussed or required.

Table 2.1   Comparison of requirements for *documented procedures.*

BSR/ISO/ASQ Q9001-2000		ANSI/ISO/ASQC Q9001-1994	
Clause	*Documented procedure required*	*Clause*	*Documented procedure required*
		4.3.1	Contract review
		4.4.1	Design control
5.5.6	Document control	4.5.6	Document and data control
		4.6.1	Purchasing
		4.7	Customer supplied product
		4.8	Product identification and traceability
		4.9	Process control
		4.10.1	Inspection and testing
		4.11.1	Control of measuring and test equipment
		4.12	Inspection and test status
8.3	Control of nonconformity	4.13.1	Control of nonconforming product
8.5.2	Corrective action	4.14.1	Corrective and preventive action
8.5.3	Preventive action	4.15.1	Handling, storage, packaging, preservation, and delivery of product
5.5.7	Control of quality records	4.16	Control of quality records
8.2.2	Internal quality audits	4.17	Internal quality audits
		4.18	Training
		4.19	Servicing
		4.20	Statistical techniques

Table 2.2   Specific requirements for documentation other than documented procedures.

BSR/ISO/ASQ Q9001-2000 Clause	Specific Requirements for Documentation Other than Documented Procedures
4.1[1]	"The organization shall establish, document, ...a quality management system...."
4.2[1]	"...documentation shall include: a) ... b) documents required by the organization to ensure the effective operation and control of its processes...."
5.4.2[1]	"...The output of the planning shall be documented...."
5.5.3[2]	"The quality policy shall be controlled."
5.5.5[3]	"The quality manual shall be controlled."
7.1[1]	"...Planning of the realization processes shall be consistent with the other requirements of the organization's quality management system and shall be documented in a form suitable for the organization's method of operation."
7.3.2[1]	(Design) "... Inputs relating to product requirements shall be defined and documented...."
7.3.3[1]	"The outputs of the design and/or development process shall be documented...."
7.3.7[1]	"Design and/or development changes shall be identified, documented...."
7.3.7	"The results of the review of changes and subsequent follow up actions shall be documented...."
7.4.2[1]	"Purchasing documents shall contain information...ensure the adequacy of...purchasing documents prior to their release."

[1]Requirement for documentation but no direct reference to clause 5.5.6.

[2]Requirement for control referencing clause 5.5.6 but not using the term *document*.

[3]Requirement for control of the quality manual referencing clause 5.5.6. By definition, the quality manual must be documented. See clause 2.7.4 of ISO 9000:2000.

For example, in clause 5.3 there is no requirement to create a documented procedure for describing the process of creating a quality policy. However, the organization must have a quality policy, and this quality policy is a document that needs to be controlled. This means that processes must ensure that the most current version of the quality policy has been issued and that obsolete versions have been removed or appropriately marked as such. It would be confusing to have obsolete versions of an organization's quality policy still present within the organization.

Organizations have many options for documenting their system. Note, for example, that the quality manual need not be a separate document. Systems can be developed where the manual contains procedures. In fact, for a small organization it may be appropriate to include most or all of the system documentation in a single manual. Depending on the size and complexity of the organization, it may also be appropriate that the documents describing the sequences and interactions of processes be combined with the procedures that describe the system. Certainly other combinations are possible. Remember that the extent of required documentation depends on the following:

- Size and type of organization
- Complexity and interaction of the organization's processes
- Competency of the organization's people

Organizations may use any form or media for any of the documents in the quality management system. This means that the quality manual, the documented procedures and the other documents of the system may be published in any way the organization chooses; there are no restrictions. However, the organization must remember in selecting its documentation media that the document control provisions of clause 5.5.6 must be met.

DEFINITIONS

Document (2.7.1)—information and its support medium

EXAMPLES   Record, specification, drawing, report, standard.

NOTE 1   The medium may be paper, magnetic, electronic or optical computer disc, photograph or master sample, or a combination thereof.

NOTE 2   A set of documents, for example specifications and/or records, is frequently called 'documentation'.

NOTE 3   Some requirements relate to all types of documents, however there may be different requirements for specifications and records.

Procedure (2.4.8)—specified way to carry out an activity or a process

NOTE 1   Procedures may be documented or not.

NOTE 2   When a procedure is documented, the term "written procedure" or "documented procedure" is frequently used.

NOTE 3   A process where the conformity of the resulting product cannot be readily or economically verified is frequently referred to as a "special process".

Source: BSR/ISO/ASQ Q9000-2000.

 # TYPICAL AUDIT ITEMS FOR COMPLIANCE

Items representing a difference from ISO 9001:1994 have a Δ at the end.

- Have documented procedures been prepared where specifically required by ISO/DIS 9001:2000 (see Table 2.1)? Δ

- Is the extent of quality management system documentation dependent on the size and type of the organization? Δ

- Is the extent of quality management system documentation dependent on the complexity and interaction of processes in the organization?

- Is the extent of quality management system documentation dependent on the competence of personnel in the organization?

CHAPTER

3

Management Responsibility

5 Management responsibility

5.1 Management commitment

Top management shall provide evidence of its commitment to the development and improvement of the quality management system by:

a) communicating to the organization the importance of meeting customer as well as regulatory and legal requirements;

b) establishing the quality policy and quality objectives;

c) conducting management reviews;

d) ensuring the availability of necessary resources.

5.2 Customer focus

Top management shall ensure that customer needs and expectations are determined, converted into requirements and fulfilled with the aim of achieving customer satisfaction.

NOTE When determining customer needs and expectations, it is important to consider obligations related to product, including regulatory and legal requirements (see 7.2.1).

Source: BSR/ISO/ASQ Q9001-2000.

 Top management commitment is now required not only to develop the quality management system but also to continually improve it.

Top management is required to demonstrate commitment by conducting specific activities. It is not sufficient for top managers to only claim commitment. There are specific responsibilities that must be fulfilled. Some of these responsibilities were required of top managers by the 1994 version of ISO 9001; others may well have been delegated. As with the 1994 version, top management must provide resources and must perform management reviews. They must also be actively involved in the planning necessary to establish the quality policy and objectives. Active participation of senior leaders in the development and deployment of both the quality policy and related objectives is a must for attaining compliance.

 ISO/DIS 9001:2000 does have two new requirements in this clause. In addition to communicating the organization's policy and goals as required by the 1994 version, top management must communicate to the organization the importance of meeting customer requirements and regulatory and legal requirements. There must be a process not only to create awareness of the organization's quality policy and quality objectives but also to maintain this awareness. Leaders demonstrate this commitment by both words and actions.

 Top management must ensure that customer needs and expectations are determined and converted into internal requirements. It is also top management's responsibility to make certain that customer requirements are understood and met. Top management is not expected to accomplish all of this. They must be able to demonstrate that they have put in place processes to make certain that these requirements are met.

 ## DEFINITIONS

Customer (2.3.5)—organization or person that receives a product

EXAMPLES   Consumer, client, end-user, retailer, beneficiary and purchaser.
NOTE   A supplier can be internal or external to the customer's organization.

Management system (2.2.2)—system to establish policy and objectives and to achieve those objectives

NOTE   A management system of an organization may include different management systems, such as a quality management system, a financial management system, or an environmental management system.

Organization (2.3.1)—group of people and facilities with an orderly arrangement of responsibilities, authorities and relationships

EXAMPLES   Company, corporation, firm, enterprise, institution, charity, sole trader, association, or parts or combination thereof.

NOTE 1   An organization can be incorporated, public or private.

NOTE 2   This definition is valid for the purposes of quality management systems standards. The term "organization" is defined differently in ISO/IEC Guide 2.

Quality (2.1.1)—ability of a set of inherent characteristics of a product, system or process to fulfil requirements of customers and other interested parties

NOTE   The term "quality" may be used with adjectives such as poor, good or excellent.

Quality management system (2.2.3)—system to establish a quality policy and quality objectives and to achieve those objectives

Top management (2.2.7)—person or group of people who direct or control an organization at the highest level

Source: BSR/ISO/ASQ Q9000-2000.

 # CONSIDERATIONS FOR DOCUMENTATION

Although not specifically required, organizations should consider documenting their process to communicate customer, regulatory, and legal requirements. This clause does not require any specific quality records.

 # TYPICAL AUDIT ITEMS FOR COMPLIANCE

Items representing a difference from ISO 9001:1994 have a Δ at the end.

- Has top management established quality policy?
- Has top management developed quality objectives?
- Do top managers regularly perform management reviews, and are results against quality objectives regularly included in such reviews?

- Does top management provide and regularly review the adequacy of resources?

- Is there a process to ensure employees understand the importance of fulfilling customer, regulatory, and legal requirements? Δ

5.3 Quality policy

Top management shall ensure that the quality policy:

a) is appropriate to the purpose of the organization;

b) includes a commitment to meeting requirements and to continual improvement;

c) provides a framework for establishing and reviewing quality objectives;

d) is communicated and understood at appropriate levels in the organization;

e) is reviewed for continuing suitability.

The quality policy shall be controlled (see 5.5.6).

Source: BSR/ISO/ASQ Q9001-2000.

Clause 5.1 requires that top management establish the quality policy. Clause 5.3 elaborates on the substance of the policy. The clause has three requirements for the content of the policy itself and two requirements that deal with how it is to be communicated and reviewed.

The policy must first be appropriate to the needs of the organization and its customers. This means that the organization should not adopt a policy that it cannot carry out. In other words, the organization must have both the capability and the dedication required to actually implement the policy. It will do no good to create a policy with lofty goals if it is impossible for the organization to meet those goals. On the other hand, the policy must also meet the needs of the organization's customers, which is a basic concept of ISO 9001. In developing the policy, it is important to think through the elements of policy needed to meet customer needs. The needs can then be defined in terms of the key processes or activities of the organization.

 Clause 5.3 has two basic requirements that the actual policy must meet. It must include commitment to meeting requirements and commitment to continual improvement. Although meeting requirements was a fundamental of ISO 9001:1994, specific reference to continual improvement of the quality management system is new. Meeting requirements and continual improvement are foundations of the system, and there must be a commitment to both of these concepts.

There is a new emphasis on *continual improvement of the quality management system.* Improvement is not new; the 1994 version of ISO 9001 has requirements to use corrective and preventive actions as a means for improvement, and these concepts are retained. With ISO/DIS 9001:2000, the organization must plan its activities for improvement and the measurable objectives of the organization must be set with improvement in mind. Measurement, collection, and analysis of data are required as methods for identifying areas for improvement. This process of improving the effectiveness of meeting the requirements of the quality management system must be done on a continual basis through methods such as periodic management reviews.

 The quality policy must create the framework for setting and reviewing objectives, and the framework should be appropriate to the needs of the organization. It must also provide for the establishment of objectives at the various levels and functions of the organization. The standard requires this to be done at "each relevant" function and level. Organizations need to define what this means for them. In making this determination, organizations need to consider their own needs and those of their customers. The relevance of having an objective at any particular organizational level or function is left to the organization to determine.

Once established, the organization must deploy the policy. This means it must be communicated to all involved in ways that are understandable. Understanding of the policy implies that each individual in the organization knows his or her role in carrying out the policy. This is much more than being able to quote what the policy says; members of the organization should clearly understand their roles in ensuring that the policy is implemented.

The policy must also be reviewed to ensure its continuing suitability. This review should be conducted at a time and in a manner that best suits the organization's needs. If goals and objectives are tightly tied to the policy, then the review can actually become an ongoing activity. In some organizations it might be more appropriate for the policy to be reviewed periodically as part of a strategic planning process or as part of management review. In any event, the policy should not be considered to be static but rather to be evolving as the organization, its customers, and its products change over time.

.The objectives need not be included in the policy itself, but the policy must provide some basis for establishing and reviewing them.

ISO 9001:1994 required that policy be relevant to the expectations and needs of customers. ISO/DIS 9001:2000 goes further by mandating commitment to meeting requirements. The requirements include those of the organization itself, any applicable regulatory requirements, and customer-specified requirements. Requirements also include those derived from customer expectations and needs that may not have been directly stated or specified by the customer.

Some organizations have dynamic quality policies that actually include the objectives and numerical goals for overall organizational performance. Because the goals change from time to time, this type of policy must be updated frequently, offering a clear opportunity to validate the objectives and commitment components of the policy.

Other organizations find inclusion of objectives in the policy to be cumbersome. It is important for each organization to find a method of developing, deploying, and reviewing the quality policy that fits its needs.

The notes to the definition of quality policy in ISO 9000 provide some insight into policy development. These notes are informative and, thus, they do not form part of the requirements.

Organizations wanting successful quality management systems should align the quality policy with the overall strategies and needs of their business. Organizations should consider the eight quality management principles stated in ISO/DIS 9000:2000 as input to policy development. It is important to understand that these principles were input for developing the ISO 9000:2000 family of standards. These eight quality management principles are not a part of the requirements of ISO/DIS 9001:2000 and should never be used as a basis for compliance audits to ISO/DIS 9001:2000.

 # DEFINITIONS

Quality policy (2.2.4)—overall intentions and directions of an organization related to quality as formally expressed by top management

NOTE 1   The quality policy should be consistent with the overall policy and provide a framework for the setting of quality objectives

NOTE 2   Quality management principles of this International Standard may form a basis for the establishment of a quality policy.

Quality requirement (2.1.3)—requirement for inherent characteristics of a product, process or system

NOTE   Inherent characteristics are part of the product, process or system (e.g. technical characteristics like the diameter of a bolt, the production rate of a machine, the waiting time at a call centre). Assigned characteristics (e.g. the price of a product) are not inherent characteristics.

Requirement (2.1.2)—need or expectation that is stated, customarily implied or obligatory

NOTE 1   A qualifier may be used to denote a specific type of requirement, e.g. product requirement, quality system requirement, customer requirement.

NOTE 2   A specified requirement is one which is stated, for example, in a document.

NOTE 3   Requirements may be generated by different interested parties.

Source: BSR/ISO/ASQ Q9000-2000.

TYPICAL AUDIT ITEMS FOR COMPLIANCE

Items representing a difference from ISO 9001:1994 have a Δ at the end.

- Has a quality policy been developed?
- Does the quality policy include commitment to meeting requirements and commitment to continual improvement? Δ
- Does the quality policy provide a framework for establishing and reviewing the quality objectives? Δ
- Are quality objectives quantified? Δ
- Has top management determined that the quality policy meets the needs of the organization and its customers?
- Is the policy communicated to and understood by all in the organization?
- Are the members of the organization clear as to their role in carrying out the policy? Δ
- Is the quality policy included in the document control process? Δ
- Is the quality policy reviewed for continuing suitability? Δ

5.4 Planning

5.4.1 Quality objectives

Top management shall ensure that quality objectives are established at relevant functions and levels within the organization. The quality objectives shall be measurable and consistent with the quality policy including the commitment to continual improvement. Quality objectives shall include those needed to meet requirements for product (see 7.1).

5.4.2 Quality planning

Top management shall ensure that the resources needed to achieve the quality objectives are identified and planned. The output of the planning shall be documented.

Quality planning shall include:

a) the processes of the quality management system, considering permissible exclusions (see 1.2);

b) the resources needed;

c) continual improvement of the quality management system.

Planning shall ensure that change is conducted in a controlled manner and that the integrity of the quality management system is maintained during this change.

Source: BSR/ISO/ASQ Q9001-2000.

The quantification of objectives implied in ISO 9001:1994 is now a specific requirement. Clause 5.4.1 requires that objectives be measurable. In many organizations, quality objectives are quantitative targets or goals. Where more abstract statements are used as quality objectives, organizations may need to review them to ensure they are measurable. Objectives at the operational level at least are required to be quantitative. The second note in the ISO/DIS 9000:2000 definition of a quality objective states that at the operational level, objectives should be quantitative. Thus, objectives may be stated in any form suitable to the circumstances but eventually should be quantified so that performance can be measured. Many organizations find that quantifiable objectives are a useful tool in achieving conformity and continual improvement. It should also be noted that the definition notes are careful to point out that the term *objective* is to be interpreted broadly to be the same as *goal, target,* or *aim*.

The organization must include the objectives needed to meet the requirements for the products and/or services. To set such objectives, there must be an understanding of the processes that are important in meeting requirements. Key process outputs that are important to the customer must be identified, and the processes that create those outputs must be understood. This basic process information can be used as the first step in determining the important objectives. To determine lower level objectives, *relevant* processes can then be broken down so that the key objectives can be defined at each organizational level and function. As the objectives flow through the levels and functions of the organization, they may take on different terms so that a number of lower level objectives may be needed to support a higher level objective.

There is also a requirement that the objectives be consistent with continual improvement of the quality management system. Where output does not meet customer requirements, targeting quality management system improvements and setting objectives for improved capability of the quality management system can lead to improved effectiveness in achieving an acceptable level of performance. Where output meets customer needs, the objectives may relate to maintaining or improving the system so that the customer needs can be met more rapidly or with fewer in-process defects.

Once objectives have been set, the organization must identify and plan the resources needed to achieve them. The planning must determine and document the activities and associated resources required to meet objectives. This includes identification and planning of the quality management system processes and the interaction among those processes. Basic product-realization processes should be identified and understood in sufficient detail to plan the quality management system. Planning of product-realization processes is a separate concept and is covered in clause 7.1.

 Planning must include requirements for continual improvement, which are specified in clause 8.1. This means that the measurement, analysis, and review processes needed for continual improvement of the quality management system must be identified. The concept of planned continual improvement is new with ISO/DIS 9001:2000. Although ISO 9001:1994 required the organization to take corrective and preventive actions in order to promote improvement, there was no requirement that the improvement activities be planned.

Resource needs must be determined, and this determination is best made based on an understanding of the processes necessary to operate and improve the quality management system.

 Clause 8.1 also requires management of change so that integrity of the quality management system is maintained when changes occur in the organization. Changes can include organizational structure, turnover of personnel, or significant increases or decreases in volume. The organization should have a basic process to deal with these types of changes as they occur. The process should provide for addressing quality management system implications of

change. The details of dealing with any specific change will require specific decisions at the time, but the basic process should be worked out as part of quality system planning. This process must include identification of changes and implications as an input to management reviews.

 The specific requirement for controlling change and maintaining the integrity of the quality management system during change is new. This means that the quality management system must be a key consideration each time the organization embarks on reorganization, process improvement, or other changes. Since we live in an era of constant change, this is a very important concept to understand. It is not intended that the requirements prevent change; rather, organizations must conduct change activities in a controlled manner that does not negatively impact the quality management system.

SERVICES

In the planning process, service organizations should consider the differences in setting objectives for the parts of the organization that provide service in direct contact with the customer. Objectives that relate to levels of service performance can sometimes be established between the organization and the customer. Defining the key processes that actually create the service for the customer can help in determination of the objectives.

HARDWARE, SOFTWARE, AND PROCESSED MATERIALS

While the most important objectives may relate directly to the organization's hardware, software, or processed materials, there may be other aspects of the customers' needs (such as delivery timing, customer service, or price) that are equally important and should not be ignored in determining objectives.

DEFINITIONS

Process (2.4.1)—system of activities which uses resources to transform inputs into outputs

NOTE 1   Inputs to a process are typically outputs of other processes.

NOTE 2   Processes in an organization typically are planned and carried out under controlled conditions to add value.

NOTE 3   A process where the conformity of the resulting product cannot be readily or economically verified is frequently referred to as a "special process".

Quality objective (2.2.5)—something sought, or aimed at, related to quality

NOTE 1   Quality objectives should be based on the organization's quality policy.

NOTE 2   Quality objectives typically are specified at different levels in the organization. At an operational level, quality objectives should be quantitative.

NOTE 3   Different terms are sometimes used for quality objectives, such as quality targets, quality aims, or quality goals.

Quality planning (2.2.9)—part of quality management focused on setting quality objectives and specifying necessary operational processes and related resources to fulfill quality objectives

NOTE   Establishing quality plans may be part of quality planning

Source: BSR/ISO/ASQ Q9000-2000.

 CONSIDERATIONS FOR DOCUMENTATION

ISO/DIS 9001:2000 does not require specific documented procedures for this clause, but it does require that the output of quality planning be documented. The processes of the quality management system can be documented with flowcharts, in the quality manual, or in separate procedures. Resources can be identified in the minutes of meetings. Since planning is a dynamic activity, it would be expected that these documents be updated periodically. In addition, the requirements of clause 4.2, *General documentation requirements,* state that where specific documented procedures are required in this international standard, the organization must determine what is required to "ensure the effective operation and control of its processes." The quality manual or other procedures should discuss how the planning activities take place and how planning is periodically updated. This clause does not require any specific quality records.

 ## TYPICAL AUDIT ITEMS FOR COMPLIANCE

Items representing a difference from ISO 9001:1994 have a Δ at the end.

- Have quality objectives been established at each relevant function and level in the organization? Δ
- Do quality objectives include those needed to meet requirements for the organization's products and/or services?
- Has the organization identified the activities and processes required to meet objectives? Quality management system processes? Product and/or service-realization processes? Verification processes? Permissible exclusions? Δ
- Does quality planning include continual improvement of the quality management system? Δ
- Does quality planning include resources? Δ
- Does quality planning take into account the needs of the organization as changes occur? Δ

5.5 Administration.

5.5.1 General

The following clauses describe the administration of the quality management system

5.5.2 Responsibility and authority

Functions and their interrelations within the organization, including responsibilities and authorities, shall be defined and communicated in order to facilitate effective quality management.

5.5.3 Management Representative

Top management shall appoint member(s) of the management who, irrespective of other responsibilities, shall have responsibility and authority that includes:

a) ensuring that processes of the quality management system are established and maintained;

b) reporting to top management on the performance of the quality management system, including needs for improvement;

c) promoting awareness of customer requirements throughout the organization.

NOTE The responsibility of a management representative may include liaison with external parties on matters relating to the quality management system.

5.5.4 Internal communication

The organization shall ensure communication between its various levels and functions regarding the processes of the quality management system and their effectiveness.

Source: BSR/ISO/ASQ Q9001-2000.

The various roles of personnel in the organization must be defined so that their responsibility, authority, and interactions are clear. These roles must be communicated clearly to all in the organization who have a need to know them. This type of clarity is important for all key personnel involved with the quality management system. This was a fundamental in ISO 9001:1994. ISO/DIS 9001:2000 goes further by requiring that *functions* and their *interrelationships* within the organization be defined and communicated. Organization charts are frequently used as one way of documenting and communicating responsibility, authority, and interactions of personnel.

It is especially important to make clear the authority and responsibilities of those in the organization who must be free to identify nonconformities and to require that corrective action be taken. This type of activity can involve anyone from senior managers to production workers depending on the organization's size, complexity, and operating philosophy.

There is also a specific requirement that top management appoint one or more members of the organization's management as a *management representative*. Management representatives must fulfill specific duties, including the following:

- They must ensure that the quality management system is implemented and maintained in accordance with ISO 9001. The representatives act as a link with top management and ensure the system's status and improvement needs are communicated to top management. Normally it is the management representative who acts as the primary interface individual with outside parties in relation to the quality management system. This often includes interaction with, for example, customer representatives or third-party auditing organizations.

 - They must ensure that there is awareness of customer requirements throughout the organization. This means that there must be a process for communication of customer requirements. The management representative has flexibility in determining how to address this requirement.

Since there are situations where a single management representative is not practical, BSR/ISO/ASQ Q9001-2000 makes it clear that an organization may appoint more than one representative. Organizations should consider the appointments very carefully.

   Although adequate communication has always been key to successful quality management system implementation, the requirement related to internal communications is new with ISO/DIS 9001:2000. Earlier drafts of ISO/DIS 9001:2000 contained a requirement for a procedure to cover internal communications. This has been dropped and has been replaced with a requirement that adequate communications take place regarding the processes of the system. These communications can take place in any manner that best suits the needs of the organization.

 DEFINITIONS

Customer (2.3.5)—organization or person that receives a product

EXAMPLES   Consumer, client, end-user, retailer, beneficiary and purchaser.
NOTE   A supplier can be internal or external to the customer's organization.

Requirement (2.1.2)—need or expectation that is stated, customarily implied or obligatory

NOTE 1   A qualifier may be used to denote a specific type of requirement, e.g. product requirement, quality system requirement, customer requirement.
NOTE 2   A specified requirement is one which is stated, for example, in a document.
NOTE 3   Requirements may be generated by different interested parties.

Top management (2.2.7)—person or group of people who direct or control an organization at the highest level

Source: BSR/ISO/ASQ Q9000-2000.

TYPICAL AUDIT ITEMS FOR COMPLIANCE

Items representing a difference from ISO 9001:1994 have a Δ at the end.

- Are the organization's functions defined and communicated to facilitate effective quality management?
- Are responsibilities and authorities defined and communicated to facilitate effective quality management?
- Has top management appointed one or more management representatives as appropriate? Δ
- Has top management defined the responsibilities and authority of the management representative?
- Does the management representative ensure that the processes of the quality management system are established and maintained? How?
- Does the management representative report to top management on the performance of the quality management system?
- Does the management representative promote awareness of customer requirements throughout the organization? Δ
- Do discussions with employees at all levels indicate that the organization effectively communicates processes of the quality management system and their effectiveness? Δ

5.5.5 Quality manual

A quality manual shall be established and maintained that includes the following:

a) the scope of the quality management system, including details of, and justification for, any exclusions(see 1.2.);

b) documented procedures or reference to them;

c) a description of the sequence and interaction of the processes included in the quality management system.

The quality manual shall be controlled (see 5.5.6).

NOTE The quality manual may be part of the overall documentation of the organization.

Source: BSR/ISO/ASQ Q9001-2000.

The quality manual is the document that describes the overall quality management system, its processes, and the interrelationship among those processes. As we discussed in chapter 2, the manual can either contain or reference more detailed documented procedures. The manual should be useful to facilitate understanding of the quality management system, and the organization should not feel constrained to a specific format for the manual's content. The format and content should be developed in a way that describes how the organization's quality management system *really* works.

While ISO 9001:1994 required a description of how the system is documented, ISO/DIS 9001:2000 requires the manual to have a description of the "sequence and interaction" of processes that make up the system. Note this difference in focus.

There is a new requirement in clause 5.5.5a that the quality manual include the scope of the quality management system, including the details of and justification for each exclusion the organization has taken under clause 1.2, *Permissible exclusions*.

 ## DEFINITIONS

Quality (2.1.2)—ability of a set of inherent characteristics of a product, system or process to fulfil requirements of customers and other interested parties

NOTE   The term "quality" may be used with adjectives such as poor, good or excellent.

Quality management system (2.2.3)—system to establish a quality policy and quality objectives and to achieve those objectives

Quality manual (2.7.4)—document specifying the quality management system (2.2.3) of an organization

NOTE   Quality manuals may vary in detail and format to suit the size and complexity of an individual organization.

Source: BSR/ISO/ASQ Q9000-2000.

 ## TYPICAL AUDIT ITEMS FOR COMPLIANCE

Items representing a difference from ISO 9001:1994 have a Δ at the end.

- Does the organization have a quality manual that describes the sequence and interaction of the processes in the quality management system? Δ

- Does the quality manual either include or reference the documented procedures describing the processes of the quality management system?

- Does the quality manual include the scope of the quality management system, including details of and justification for any exclusions taken under clause 1.2? Δ

- Is the quality manual a controlled document?

5.5.6 Control of documents

Documents required for the quality management system shall be controlled. A documented procedure shall be established:

a) to approve documents for adequacy prior to issue;

b) to review, update as necessary and re-approve documents;

c) to identify the current revision status of documents;

d) to ensure that relevant versions of applicable documents are available at points of use;

e) to ensure that documents remain legible, readily identifiable and retrievable;

f) to ensure that documents of external origin are identified and their distribution controlled;

g) to prevent the unintended use of obsolete documents, and to apply suitable identification to them if they are retained for any purpose.

Documents defined as quality records shall be controlled (see 5.5.7).

5.5.7 Control of quality records

Records required for the quality management system shall be controlled. Such records shall be maintained to provide evidence of conformance to requirements and of effective operation of the quality management system. A documented procedure shall be established for the identification, storage, retrieval, protection, retention time and disposition of quality records.

Source: BSR/ISO/ASQ Q9001-2000.

Documents that are part of the quality management system must be controlled to ensure correct requirements are available. Controls for documents must include a number of specific activities.

Approval prior to issue for use is required to ensure that documents are adequate. The document control procedure should specify how this approval is accomplished. Many organizations find it worthwhile to include a process for internal review of the documents by all affected units of the organizations as part of the preissue review process.

Review, updating, and reapproval is required as necessary. ISO 9001:1994 had a requirement related to changes in documents, which required that changes be reviewed and reapproved. ISO/DIS 9001:2000 adds the concept that the documents themselves must be reviewed. Some organizations create systems to ensure that documents are reviewed for continued suitability on a periodic, scheduled basis. There is no stated requirement that the review be periodic or scheduled, just that it occur as necessary. If the documentation system is vibrant and its documents are actively used on a daily basis, it may prove sufficient to conduct the reviews only when there is a known need to make a change. Each organization should define a document review, revision, and reapproval process that suits its own business needs.

Controls are required to ensure that the correct revisions of documents are identified and available at the points of use, including controls (such as identification) to prevent unintended use of obsolete documents. Many organizations have migrated to computer-based processes for tracking the current issue of documents.

Means are required to ensure documents remain legible, retrievable, and readily identifiable.

Controls must extend to documents of external origin such as industry and customer specifications and standards.

Records are a special type of document, and they have their own control requirements. Records are documents that provide evidence that an activity has been accomplished or that an event has happened. Records are also used to provide information on the condition (such as conformity or nonconformity) of a product. While the other types of documents in the quality management system may indicate what is to be done (the current and future action), records provide evidence of what has occurred (past action).

As with documented procedures, there has been a shift in the emphasis of the record requirements. ISO/DIS 9001:2000 has somewhat more emphasis on the organization defining the records that are required rather than specifying them in the standards. Table 3.1 gives a listing of the specified record requirements as well as the requirements for the organization to identify its own record needs.

Table 3.1 Record-related requirements.

BSR/ISO/ASQ Q9001-2000		ANSI/ISO/ASQC Q9001-1994	
Clause	Record-related requirement	Clause	Record-related requirement
5.6.3	Management review	4.1.3	Management review
		4.16*	Retention times of quality records…recorded
6.2	Education, experience, training, and qualifications		
		4.18	Records of training
7.1d**	The records that are necessary to provide confidence of conformity of the processes and resulting product	4.16**	Records shall be maintained to demonstrate conformance to specified requirements and the effective operation of the quality system; pertinent quality records from the subcontractor shall be an element of these data
		4.2.3h	Identification of records required during the quality planning
		4.10.1**	Records to be established shall be detailed in the quality plan or documented procedures

(Continued)

BSR/ISO/ASQ Q9001-2000		ANSI/ISO/ASQC Q9001-1994	
Clause	Record-related requirement	Clause	Record-related requirement
		4.10.5**	Establish and maintain records that provide evidence that the product has been inspected and/or tested
7.2.2	Review of customer requirements	4.3.4	Records of contract review
7.3.4	Results of the design and development reviews and subsequent follow-up actions	4.4.6	Records of design reviews
7.3.5	The results of the design and/or development verification and subsequent follow-up actions shall be recorded	4.4.7	The design-verification measures shall be recorded
7.3.6	Results of the design and/or development validation and subsequent follow-up actions		
7.4.2	Results of evaluations of supplier and follow-up actions shall be recorded	4.6.2c	Establish and maintain quality records of acceptable subcontractors
		4.10.2.3	Incoming product is released for urgent production purposes; prior to verification, it shall be positively identified and recorded
7.5.2	The unique identification of the product, where traceability is a requirement	4.8	Unique identification of individual product or batches, where traceability is a requirement

(Continued)

Table 3.1 Continued.

BSR/ISO/ASQ Q9001-2000		ANSI/ISO/ASQC Q9001-1994	
Clause	Record-related requirement	Clause	Record-related requirement
7.5.3*	Occurrence of any customer property that is lost, damaged, or otherwise found to be unsuitable	4.7	Any customer or supplier product that is lost, damaged, or is otherwise unsuitable for use shall be recorded and reported to the customer
7.5.5d**	Requirements for records related to process validation	4.9	Records shall be maintained for qualified processes, equipment, and personnel, as appropriate
		4.11.1	Shall maintain records as evidence of control of calibration checks
7.6a*	The basis used for calibration		
7.6d	Results of calibration	4.11.2e	Calibration records for inspection, measuring, and test equipment
		4.11.2d*	Suitable indicator or approved identification record to show calibration status
8.2.2**	Recording audit results	4.17	Results of the audits shall be recorded
8.2.2**	Follow-up audit actions include reporting of verification results	4.17	Follow-up audit activities shall verify and record the implementation and effectiveness of the corrective action taken

(Continued)

BSR/ISO/ASQ Q9001-2000		ANSI/ISO/ASQC Q9001-1994	
Clause	*Record-related requirement*	*Clause*	*Record-related requirement*
8.2.4	Evidence of conformity with the acceptance criteria; records shall indicate the authority responsible for release of product	4.10.5	Records shall identify the inspection authority responsible for the release of product
8.3**	Report proposed rectification of nonconforming product to customer if required	4.13.2	Description of nonconformity that has been accepted by customer and description of repairs shall be recorded to denote the actual condition
		4.14.1*	Record any changes to the documented procedures resulting from corrective and preventive action
		4.14.2b	Investigation of the cause of nonconformities relating to product, process, and quality system and recording the results of the investigation
8.5.2e**	Record results of corrective actions taken		
8.5.3c**	Record results of preventive actions taken		

*Apparent direct requirement for a record but no reference to clause 5.5.7 of BSR/ISO/ASQ Q9001-2000 or clause 4.16 of ANSI/ISO/ASQC Q9001-1994

**Not a specific record requirement; rather, a requirement for a process or procedure to define records to be kept; no reference to clause 5.5.7 of BSR/ISO/ASQ Q9001-2000 or clause 4.16 of ANSI/ISO/ASQC Q9001-1994

Organizations must identify the records to be retained along with the length of time each type of record must be retained. Many organizations do not have lengthy retention times and need only provide for the normal filing of records. In such cases, the procedure can be very simple with a matrix giving the information required. Other organizations have very long retention times for some records and need to consider long-term indexing and retrieval from off-site archives. For all cases, controls should be appropriate to the circumstances and the retention times needed.

Organizations also need to identify the storage conditions and protection required for the records that they maintain. It is particularly important to consider how the organization would be affected if the records became lost or were destroyed. Organizations should look at each type of record and determine appropriate protection based on criticality to the continued operations of the quality management system. For many noncritical records, storage in normal file cabinets may be appropriate. Critical records should be considered for protection from potential fire and other damage. Provisions need to be made for backup of records stored on magnetic media and for appropriate protection of the backup copies. In the event of a fire, it will do little good to have computer backup files stored on a shelf next to the computer.

 DEFINITIONS

Document (2.7.1)—information and its support medium

EXAMPLES   Record (2.7.6), specification (2.7.2), drawing, report, standard.
NOTE 1   The medium may be paper, magnetic, electronic or optical computer disc, photograph or master sample, or a combination thereof.
NOTE 2   A set of documents, for example specifications and/or records, is frequently called 'documentation'.
NOTE 3   Some requirements (2.1.2) relate to all types of documents, however there may be different requirements for specifications and records.

Procedure (2.4.8)—specified way to carry out an activity or a process

NOTE 1   Procedures may be documented or not.
NOTE 2   When a procedure is documented, the term "written procedure" or "documented procedure" is frequently used.

Quality (2.1.1)—ability of a set of inherent characteristics of a product, system or process to fulfil requirements of customers and other interested parties

NOTE   The term "quality" may be used with adjectives such as poor, good or excellent.

Quality management system (2.2.3)—system to establish a quality policy and quality objectives and to achieve those objectives

Requirement (2.1.1)—need or expectation that is stated, customarily implied or obligatory

NOTE 1   A qualifier may be used to denote a specific type of requirement, e.g. product requirement, quality system requirement, customer requirement.
NOTE 2   A specified requirement is one which is stated, for example, in a document.
NOTE 3   Requirements may be generated by different interested parties.

Record (2.7.6)—document stating results achieved or providing evidence of activities performed

NOTE   Quality records may be used to document traceability and to provide evidence of verification, preventive action and corrective action.

Review (2.8.6)—activity undertaken to ensure the suitability, adequacy, effectiveness and efficiency of the subject matter to achieve established objectives

EXAMPLES   Management review, design and development review, review of customer requirements and nonconformity review.

Source: BSR/ISO/ASQ Q9000-2000.

 # CONSIDERATIONS FOR DOCUMENTATION

There must be a procedure to describe how document control is accomplished, and it must include the requirements of clause 5.5.6a through clause 5.5.6g. There also must be a documented procedure for control of quality records covering the items listed in clause 5.5.7. Since control considerations for records are different from those for other documents, a separate procedure is required for control of records.

TYPICAL AUDIT ITEMS FOR COMPLIANCE

Items representing a difference from ISO 9001:1994 have a Δ at the end.

Audit items related to control of documents (except quality records)

- Has a documented procedure been established for document control?
- Are documents approved for adequacy prior to use?
- Are documents reviewed and updated as necessary? Δ
- Are document changes reapproved to ensure adequacy prior to use?
- Is current document-revision status maintained?
- Are relevant versions of applicable documents available at points of use?
- Is there a process to ensure that documents remain legible, readily identifiable, and retrievable?
- Are documents of external origin identified and controlled?
- Are obsolete documents retained for any purpose suitably identified to prevent unintended use?

Audit items related to control of quality records

- Is there a documented procedure for control of quality records?
- Have the organization's quality records been identified?
- Have retention times and disposition requirements been determined for all quality records?
- Are records disposed of as required by the organization's procedures?
- Have storage and retrieval requirements been determined and implemented for all quality records?
- Have protection requirements been determined and implemented for all quality records?

5.6 Management review

5.6.1 General

Top management shall review the quality management system, at planned intervals, to ensure its continuing suitability, adequacy and effectiveness. The review shall evaluate the need for changes to the organization's quality management system, including quality policy and quality objectives.

5.6.2 Review input

Inputs to management review shall include current performance and improvement opportunities related to the following:

a) results of audits;

b) customer feedback;

c) process performance and product conformance;

d) status of preventive and corrective actions;

e) follow-up actions from earlier management reviews;

f) changes that could affect the quality management system.

5.6.3 Review output

The outputs from the management review shall include actions related to:

a) improvement of the quality management system and its processes;

b) improvement of product related to customer requirements;

c) resource needs.

Results of management reviews shall be recorded (see 5.5.7).

Source: BSR/ISO/ASQ Q9001-2000.

Management review of the quality system is the responsibility of top management. This is no different than the requirement of ISO 9001-1994. ISO 9001-1994 also required review at defined intervals of the continuing suitability and effectiveness of the system in meeting the standard, the organization's quality policy, and objectives.

ISO/DIS 9001:2000 contains additional requirements by specifying minimum review input items and output actions. The intent is generally the same as it was with ISO 9001: 1994, and many organizations will have already structured a management review process that complies with the new requirements. But the wording of the new standard is much more prescriptive. Inputs for the reviews must now include customer feedback, process and product performance, status of preventive and corrective actions, changes that could affect the quality management system, and the results of audits. In addition, there is now a requirement to review follow-up actions from earlier management reviews.

Outputs of the management review are also specified and must include the following three specific types of actions:

- Management reviews must identify opportunities to improve the quality management system and its processes. These could include actions to simplify or foolproof processes, to develop improved methods, to improve documentation, and so on.

- "Improvement of product related to customer requirements" . . . This phrase is important—there is no requirement to improve the product beyond the point where all customer requirements are met. Improvements related to customer requirements could be items related to improved conformity with known requirements. On the other hand, remember that the top management is required in clause 5.2 to ". . . ensure that customer needs and expectations are determined, converted into requirements and fulfilled. . . ." It is important to recognize that these customer needs and expectations may change frequently so that organizations may also identify new customer requirements and establish actions to meet them.

- Actions related to resource needs, which would include ensuring that resources are provided as needed for continual operation and improvement of the quality management system.

 # DEFINITIONS

Customer (2.3.5)—organization or person that receives a product

EXAMPLES   Consumer, client, end-user, retailer, beneficiary and purchaser.
NOTE   A supplier can be internal or external to the customer's organization.

Effectiveness (2.2.13)—measure of the extent to which planned activities are realized and planned results achieved

Product (2.4.2)—result of a process

NOTE   There are four agreed generic product categories:
—hardware (e.g. engine mechanical part)
—software (e.g. computer program)
—services (e.g. transport)
—processed materials (e.g. lubricant)
Hardware and processed materials are generally tangible products, while software or services are generally intangible.
Most products comprise elements belonging to different generic product categories. Whether the product is then called hardware, processed material, software or service depends on the dominant element.
EXAMPLES   The offered product "car" consists of hardware (e.g. the tyres), processed materials (e.g. fuel, cooling liquid), software (e.g. engine control software, the driver's manual), and service (e.g. the payment facilities or the guaranty).

Requirement (2.1.2)—need or expectation that is stated, customarily implied or obligatory

NOTE 1   A qualifier may be used to denote a specific type of requirement, e.g. product requirement, quality system requirement, customer requirement.
NOTE 2   A specified requirement is one which is stated, for example, in a document.
NOTE 3   Requirements may be generated by different interested parties.

Review (2.8.6)—activity undertaken to ensure suitability, adequacy, effectiveness and efficiency of the subject matter to achieve established objectives

EXAMPLE   Management review, design and development review, review of customer requirements and nonconformity review.

Source: BSR/ISO/ASQ Q9000-2000.

TYPICAL AUDIT ITEMS FOR COMPLIANCE

Items representing a difference from ISO 9001:1994 have a Δ at the end.

- Does top management review the quality management system at planned intervals to ensure its continuing suitability, adequacy, and effectiveness?

- Do the management reviews include evaluation of the need for changes to the organization's quality management system, including quality policy and quality objectives?

- Does management review input include: results of audits, customer feedback, process performance, product performance, status of preventive and corrective actions, follow-up actions from earlier management reviews, and changes that could affect the quality management system? Δ

- Do outputs of management reviews include actions related to improvement of the quality management system and its processes? Δ

- Do outputs of management reviews include actions related to improvement of product related to customer requirements? Δ

- Do outputs of management reviews include resource needs? Δ

- Are results of management reviews recorded and maintained as quality records?

CHAPTER

4

Human and Other Resources

6 Resource management

6.1 Provision of resources

The organization shall determine and provide, in a timely manner, the resources needed

a) to implement and improve the processes of the quality management system, and

b) to address customer satisfaction.

Source: BSR/ISO/ASQ Q9001-2000.

The previous standard stated that resources needed to be available for generalized tasks: management, work, and verification activities, including internal audits. The requirement addresses resources needed for the entire quality management system—for implementation and improvement of the processes of the quality management system and for addressing customer satisfaction. This minimizes the misinterpretations that were evident previously. Management has always been expected to provide necessary resources to provide product that meets customer requirements. This is broader than just the *quality function* personnel or those individuals who do audits and inspections. Greater clarity to the requirements has been provided regarding the extent of the resources that should be under consideration within this clause.

This clause covers all resources necessary to fulfill the requirements of ISO/DIS 9001:2000. The standard specifies requirements for timely provision of resources needed to provide product and to address fulfilling customer requirements. By defining the scope of this clause in these terms, resource requirements of the entire quality management system are embraced.

The organization must identify what needs to be done to implement this standard. In determining the resource requirements, the organization should be specific to a level of detail that is appropriate. This usually includes detailing job responsibilities, authority, and interrelationships. Note that this is not a universal mandate. It may be an overwhelming, bureaucratic burden for a small service organization to write out every job responsibility. For larger companies, however, effective operation requires the recording of job responsibilities and the authorities for making decisions.

The term *resource* is often used in reference to personnel. In fact, this clause covers all resources necessary to fulfill the requirements of the standard. Although the standard is not specific as to what makes up these resources, normally this includes personnel, time, equipment, materials, supplies, instruments, and facilities.

The standard has a new requirement that the resources need to be determined and provided "in a timely fashion." Resources must be provided in a reasonable time frame. Just because a position has been defined or the need for a piece of equipment has been justified and approved for purchase does not mean that management has fulfilled its responsibilities. For example, jobs should not be left unfilled for indeterminate periods, and purchase orders should not be left open if there is a recognized need that has to be filled; they should be completed in a timely fashion.

 DEFINITIONS

Customer satisfaction (2.1.6)—customer's opinion of the degree to which a transaction has met the customer's needs and expectations

NOTE   A transaction is time and event specific and based on mutual needs and expectations and the communication of these between all parties concerned.

Quality management system (2.2.3)—system to establish a quality policy and quality objectives and to achieve those objectives

Process (2.4.1)—system of activities which uses resources to transform inputs into outputs

NOTE 1   Inputs to a process are typically outputs of other processes.

NOTE 2   Processes in an organization typically are planned and carried out under controlled conditions to add value.

NOTE 3   A process where the conformity of the resulting product cannot be readily or economically verified is frequently referred to as a "special process".

Source: BSR/ISO/ASQ Q9000-2000.

CONSIDERATIONS FOR DOCUMENTATION

The records that are created by the activities to fulfill the requirements of this clause may need to be controlled per clause 5.5.7, *Control of quality records.* The organization determines, in this case, whether records need to be controlled.

TYPICAL AUDIT ITEMS FOR COMPLIANCE

Items representing a difference from ISO 9001:1994 have a Δ at the end.

- Has the organization determined the resources necessary to implement the processes of the quality management system?

- Has the organization provided the resources necessary to implement the processes of the quality management system?

- Has the organization determined the resources necessary to improve the processes of the quality management system?

- Has the organization provided the resources necessary to improve the processes of the quality management system?

- Has the organization determined the resources necessary to address customer satisfaction? Δ

- Has the organization provided the resources necessary to address customer satisfaction? Δ

- Are the resources provided in a timely manner? Δ

- Does the organization define responsibility, authority, and the interrelationship of personnel required for the quality management system, including the necessary education, training, skills, and experience?

6.2 Human resources

6.2.1 Assignment of personnel

Personnel who are assigned responsibilities defined in the quality management system shall be competent on the basis of applicable education, training, skills and experience.

Source: BSR/ISO/ASQ Q9001-2000.

The requirements of the 1994 standard have been clarified. Only parts of the requirements in ANSI/ISO/ASQC Q9001-1994, clause 4.1.2.1, *Responsibility and authority,* and of ANSI/ISO/ASQC Q9001-1994, clause 4.18, *Training,* can be found here. The remaining requirements of these clauses are contained in other clauses of this standard.

The intent of the 1994 standard, in spite of the detailed listing of tasks, was to include all personnel involved in the quality management system. The new wording adds clarity to this requirement. Similar to the scope of the preceding clause on provision of resources, the BSR/ISO/ASQ Q9001-2000 requirement is intended to encompass all personnel necessary for implementing and maintaining the quality management system. Rather than attempting to list all of these separate tasks as was done in 1994, a listing that experience has shown to be incomplete and open to misunderstanding, this clause contains a broad requirement inclusive of all personnel.

Clarity is also added with respect to personnel competency. ANSI/ISO/ASQC Q9001-1994, clause 4.18, *Training,* explicitly required personnel assigned specific tasks to be qualified. Additional requirements for trained, qualified, and experienced personnel were scattered throughout the 1994 standard in various clauses, including clauses for quality systems, process control, and design and development planning. This requirement is now expressed succinctly in clause 6.

Organizations should consider that written job requirements are usually needed in order to properly assign personnel.

The requirement in clause 6.2.1 is that personnel are competent. Before the competency of employees can be assured, the organization needs to identify job requirements.

Although the quality management system extends throughout an organization, this clause does not include all personnel—even though, in principle, everyone's work affects the quality of the products supplied by the organization. With the quality management system now structured in four main clauses, it is now clear that the intent of the standard is to relate this requirement to the personnel "assigned responsibilities defined in the quality management system." This clause includes personnel involved in top management, resource management, product realization, and measurement-analysis-improvement processes. All of these personnel are required to be competent based on education, training, skills, and experience.

 DEFINITIONS

Quality management system (2.2.3)—system to establish a quality policy and quality objectives and to achieve those objectives

Source: BSR/ISO/ASQ Q9000-2000.

 CONSIDERATIONS FOR DOCUMENTATION

The records that are created by the activities to assure competency may need to be controlled per clause 5.5.7, *Control of quality records.* In this case, the organization determines whether records need to be controlled.

 TYPICAL AUDIT ITEMS FOR COMPLIANCE

- Are personnel assigned responsibilities in the quality management system competent based on education, training, skills, and experience?

> **6.2.2 Training, awareness and competency**
>
> The organization shall:
>
> a) identify competency needs for personnel performing activities affecting quality;
>
> b) provide training to satisfy these needs;
>
> c) evaluate the effectiveness of the training provided;
>
> d) ensure that its employees are aware of the relevance and importance of their activities and how they contribute to the achievement of the quality objectives;
>
> e) maintain appropriate records of education, experience, training and qualifications (see 5.5.7).

Source: BSR/ISO/ASQ Q9001-2000.

These requirements are similar to the requirements of ISO 9001:1994, clause 4.18, *Training*. There are new requirements, including a greater emphasis on competency, a requirement to evaluate the effectiveness of the training, and a requirement to ensure that employees are aware of the importance of their work.

The training of personnel is essential for the achievement of organizational objectives. This clause pertains to all personnel at all levels within the scope of this standard. It addresses all training for accomplishing assigned tasks.

The organization must identify what classroom training, seminars, on-the-job, or other training is necessary so that every employee involved in the quality management system is competent. This is not the same thing as determining job requirements. Competency may be determined by comparisons between the job requirements that define what employees must do and the qualifications of the employee. Where training is needed, it must be provided. The training process should address the competency needs of employees so that they either may become competent or are able to stay competent.

 The training should include provisions to establish and maintain employee awareness of the importance of their work and how they contribute to the quality objectives of the organization. This training should be specific so that it relates to the responsibilities of each employee.

 Evaluation of the effectiveness of training is a new requirement. It is common practice to conduct training evaluations in the following three parts:

- Evaluation of the training immediately upon completion
- Evaluation of the training received several weeks after the training
- Evaluation of the skills developed several months after the training

One approach is to have the student's supervisor evaluate the work performance related to the training, both short term and over several months. This provides input for evaluating the adequacy of the training.

 ## DEFINITIONS

Quality (2.1.1)—ability of a set of inherent characteristics of a product, system, or process to fulfil requirements of customers and other interested parties

NOTE   The term *"quality"* may be used with adjectives such as poor, good or excellent.

Effectiveness (2.2.13)—measure of the extent to which planned activities are realized and planned results achieved

Quality objective (2.2.5)—something sought, or aimed for, related to quality

NOTE 1 Quality objectives should be based on the organization's quality policy

NOTE 2 Quality objectives are specified at different levels in the organization. At an operational level, quality objectives should be quantitative.

NOTE 3 Different terms are sometimes used for quality objectives, such as quality targets, quality aims or quality goals.

Source: BSR/ISO/ASQ Q9000-2000.

CONSIDERATIONS FOR DOCUMENTATION

Often organizations will document a formal, annual training plan to address the training needs of personnel. The records dealing with personnel education, experience, training, and qualifications that are created by the activities to fulfill the requirements of this clause need to be controlled per clause 5.5.7, *Control of quality records.*

 TYPICAL AUDIT ITEMS FOR COMPLIANCE

Items representing a difference from ISO 9001:1994 have a Δ at the end.

- Does the organization identify the competency needs of the individual personnel performing activities affecting quality, including additional training needs? Δ
- Does the organization provide training to satisfy these needs?
- Does the organization evaluate the effectiveness of the provided training? Δ
- Does the organization ensure employees are aware of the relevance and importance of their activities and how they contribute to the achievement of the quality objectives? Δ
- Does the organization maintain records of education, experience, training, and qualifications?

6.3 Facilities

The organization shall identify, provide and maintain the facilities it needs to achieve the conformity of product, including:

a) workspace and associated facilities;

b) equipment, hardware and software;

c) supporting services.

Source: BSR/ISO/ASQ Q9001-2000.

There is now a clear statement that facilities and associated infrastructure elements are within the domain of this standard. Although ISO 9001:1994 does not explicitly state requirements for facilities and workspace, it has been widely understood that these were at least partially addressed in ISO 9001:1994, clause 4.9, *Control of processes,* which does require "suitable production, installation and servicing equipment." Sector-specific standards that contain additional requirements detail these additional facility requirements under clause 4.9. Common sense dictates that physical resources need to be provided for achieving the product.

Quality management system records should indicate that the requirements of this clause have been considered and addressed.

This clause is titled *Facilities,* but the requirements are much broader than the physical facility for achieving the product. Earlier drafts of this clause were titled 6.3, *Infrastructure.* It was determined that such a term would create additional confusion as to the intent of this clause. It is simpler but somewhat misleading to use *Facilities* as the title. This clause encompasses all of the physical resources necessary to achieve the product and to provide it to the customer. These are requirements for all of the resources, excluding personnel. Of course, the requirements for personnel are covered in the preceding clause on human resources. Included in this clause are requirements to identify, provide, and maintain the facilities needed to achieve conformity of product. *Facilities* is broadly defined to encompass the workspace, the equipment, and support services.

Facilities is one of the clauses under resource management. The significance of separating it from the old process control clause should be recognized. The organization must identify, provide, and maintain appropriate facilities for all of the processes within the quality management system. This goes beyond production and service operations and beyond even the realization processes to now include the management processes; other resource processes (training, in particular); and the measurement, analysis, and improvement processes.

SERVICES

The availability of appropriate physical resources is equally important in the service sector. For a warehousing organization, successful service realization is highly dependent on the availability of warehouses in the right location and with the right capabilities. Does the warehouse require air conditioning, for example? For a delivery service, the availability of delivery vehicles is critical. For a repair facility, appropriate diagnostic and repair instruments are needed. For a food service, appropriate kitchens, handling equipment, and vehicles are needed. In each case, successful service realization requires that there has been appropriate identification, provision, and maintenance of the necessary physical resources.

HARDWARE, PROCESSED MATERIALS, AND SOFTWARE

Physical resources provide the foundation for the work that is required to implement the quality management system. Design and development of new software requires appropriate workrooms, appropriate programming tools, and appropriate processors. Manufacturing computer chips requires special clean rooms. Sterilizing medical devices requires special equipment and equipment controls. Special transports are required for delivery of products such as fuel, oil, or milk. This new clause adds clarity of focus for a critical area that previously was generally assumed to be so obvious that it did not need to be identified as a unique requirement of the quality system.

 ## DEFINITIONS

Conformity (2.6.1)—fulfilment of a requirement

NOTE   This definition is consistent with ISO/IEC Guide 2 but differs from it in phrasing to fit into the ISO 9000 concepts.

Infrastructure (2.3.3)—<organization> system of permanent facilities and equipment of an organization

Source: BSR/ISO/ASQ Q9000-2000.

CONSIDERATIONS FOR DOCUMENTATION

The records that are created by the activities to fulfill the requirements of this clause may need to be controlled per clause 5.5.7, *Control of quality records*. In this case, the organization determines whether records need to be controlled.

TYPICAL AUDIT ITEMS FOR COMPLIANCE

- Does the organization identify, provide, and maintain the workspace and associated facilities it needs to achieve the conformity of product?

- Does the organization identify, provide, and maintain the equipment, hardware, and software it needs to achieve the conformity of product?

- Does the organization identify, provide, and maintain the supporting services it needs to achieve the conformity of product?

6.4 Work environment

The organization shall identify and manage the human and physical factors of the work environment needed to achieve conformity of product.

Source: BSR/ISO/ASQ Q9001-2000.

Clause 6.4 is not a new requirement. The requirement that "a suitable working environment" is controlled is contained in ISO 9001:1994, clause 4.9, *Process control*. Including the requirement for work environment in the resource management clause applies this concept to all of the processes of the quality management system needed to achieve conformity of product. This is a broader application than in 1994.

The work environment of an organization is a combination of human and physical factors. Examples of human factors in the work environment which may affect conformity of product include the following:

- Work methods
- Safety rules and guidance, including use of protective equipment
- Ergonomics

Physical factors can also impact upon the ability to achieve conforming product. It is important to control those factors that affect product quality characteristics since they have a direct impact on the ability of the product to conform to specifications.

Examples of physical factors affecting the work environment may include the following:

- Heat
- Noise
- Light
- Hygiene
- Humidity
- Cleanliness
- Vibration
- Pollution
- Air flow

If the organization determines that it is necessary to control work areas for physical factors, it is common to consider the following:

- Identify standards to be maintained.
- Assure that the facility meets the standards.
- Train personnel on standards pertaining to their work.
- Prohibit unauthorized access to the work area.
- Implement and maintain desired physical conditions.
- Maintain records of the conditions as a means of demonstrating compliance to the standards.

SERVICES

Good personal hygiene of food service and pharmacy employees, for example, is important to ensure customer product is not contaminated. It is often tightly controlled by regulatory standards.

HARDWARE AND PROCESSED MATERIALS

Physical factors of the work environment include factors such as ambient humidity and temperature in a paint shop. Control of these factors is necessary to obtain a conforming painted surface. To achieve high performance of electronic components, particle contamination needs to be kept extremely low during fabrication.

 ## DEFINITIONS

Work environment (2.3.4)—set of conditions under which a person operates

NOTE   Conditions include physical, social, psychological and environmental factors (such as temperature, recognition schemes, ergonomics and polluted atmospheres).

Conformity (2.6.1)—fulfilment of a requirement

NOTE   This definition is consistent with ISO/IEC Guide 2 but differs from it in phrasing to fit into the ISO 9000 concepts.

Source: BSR/ISO/ASQ Q9000-2000.

 ## CONSIDERATIONS FOR DOCUMENTATION

The records that are created by the activities to fulfill the requirements of this clause may need to be controlled per clause 5.5.7, *Control of quality records.* In this case, the organization determines whether records need to be controlled.

 ## TYPICAL AUDIT ITEMS FOR COMPLIANCE

- Does the organization identify the human and physical factors of the work environment needed to achieve conformity of product?
- Does the organization manage the human and physical factors of the work environment needed to achieve conformity of product?

CHAPTER

5

Planning of Realization Processes and Customer Related Processes

7 Product realization

7.1 Planning of realization processes

Product realization is that sequence of processes and sub-processes required to achieve the product. Planning of the realization processes shall be consistent with the other requirements of the organization's quality management system and shall be documented in a form suitable for the organization's method of operation.

In planning the processes for realization of product the organization shall determine the following, as appropriate:

a) quality objectives for the product, project or contract;

b) the need to establish processes and documentation, and provide resources and facilities specific to the product;

c) verification and validation activities, and the criteria for acceptability;

d) the records that are necessary to provide confidence of conformity of the processes and resulting product.

NOTE Documentation that describes how the processes of the quality management system are applied for a specific product, project or contract may be referred to as a quality plan.

Source: BSR/ISO/ASQ Q9001-2000.

Much of the content of clause 7.1 was developed from various clauses of ISO 9001:1994 (for example, clauses 4.2.3, 4.9, 4.10, 4.15, and 4.19). The requirements were generally defined more narrowly in 1994 except for the sweeping requirement in clause 4.9 that required processes that directly affect quality to be carried out under controlled conditions. Although this clause consists of only two paragraphs, it is one of the most important clauses in ISO/DIS 9001:2000. Along with clause 4.1 and clause 8, this clause provides the essence of the use of the process approach. It requires organizations to *think* about and plan all of the processes that, when linked together, will result in the delivery of products that will conform to customer requirements, create customer satisfaction, and foster continual improvement. Planning of realization processes also must be consistent with the other requirements of the quality management system and must be documented in a form that is appropriate for the organization.

The planning activity required by clause 7.1 may not be a trivial exercise. Fewer documented procedures may be required than in the past, and no specific format is dictated, but ISO/DIS 9001:2000 demands that the organization better understand the processes needed to deliver conforming products to customers. These processes must be understood not only with respect to the products themselves but also in the broader context of the objectives of the organization and any other requirements of the quality management system. The planning activity for realization processes must address the quality objectives for the product, project, or contract; the need to establish appropriate processes and documentation; the need to provide resources and facilities specific to the product; and the consideration of verification and validation activities and the criteria for acceptability. The organization is also required to determine what records are necessary to provide confidence that the processes and resulting product conform to requirements.

Many organizations will have little problem conforming to these requirements since processes and documentation already exist to address the requirements. For others, this will require some careful thought. Perhaps flowcharts and/or process mapping will be appropriate to assure all process steps are addressed in terms of the availability of documentation, facilities, personnel, and any other required resources.

 DEFINITIONS

Requirement (2.1.2)—need or expectation that is stated, customarily implied or obligatory

NOTE 1   A qualifier may be used to denote a specific type of requirement, e.g. product requirement, quality system requirement, customer requirement.

NOTE 2   A specified requirement is one which is stated, for example, in a document (2.7.1).

NOTE 3   Requirements may be generated by different interested parties (2.3.7).

Capability (2.1.7)—ability of an organization, system or process to realize a product that fulfills the requirements for that product

Quality planning (2.2.9)—part of quality management focused on setting quality objectives and specifying necessary operational processes and related resources to fulfil the quality objectives

NOTE   Establishing quality plans may be part of quality planning.

Process (2.4.1)—system of activities which uses resources to transform inputs into outputs

NOTE 1   Inputs to a process are typically outputs of other processes.

NOTE 2   Processes in an organization typically are planned and carried out under controlled conditions to add value.

NOTE 3   A process where the conformity of the resulting product cannot be readily or economically verified is frequently referred to as a "special process".

Product (2.4.2)—result of a process

NOTE   There are four agreed generic product categories: hardware (e.g. engine mechanical part); software (e.g. computer program); services (e.g. transport); processed materials (e.g. lubricant).

Hardware and processed materials are generally tangible products, while software or services are generally intangible.

Most products comprise elements belonging to different generic product categories. Whether the product is then called hardware, processed material, software (2.4.4) or service (2.4.3) depends on the dominant element.

EXAMPLES The offered product "car" consists of hardware (e.g. the tyres), processed materials (e.g. fuel, cooling liquid), software (e.g. engine control software, the driver's manual), and service (e.g. the payment facilities or the guaranty).

Service (2.4.3)—intangible product that is the result of at least one activity performed at the interface between the supplier and customer

NOTE Service may involve, for example: an activity performed on a customer-supplied tangible (e.g. the repair of a car) or intangible (e.g. the preparation of a tax return) product; the delivery of a tangible product (e.g. in the transportation industry); the delivery of an intangible product (e.g. the delivery of knowledge) or the creation of ambience for the customer (e.g. in the hospitality industry).

Software (2.4.4)—intellectual product consisting of information on a support medium

NOTE 1 Software can be in the form of concepts, transactions or procedures.
NOTE 2 A computer program is an example of software.

Source: BSR/ISO/ASQ Q9000-2000.

CONSIDERATIONS FOR DOCUMENTATION

The organization should consider preparing a documented procedure to describe how the planning is accomplished. Alternatively, this process could be described in the quality manual. Where a procedure is developed, it is recommended that standard checklists and other planning formats be developed and incorporated into the procedure. This clause also has a specific requirement that the planning define records required to provide confidence of conformity.

TYPICAL AUDIT ITEMS FOR COMPLIANCE

Items representing a difference from ISO 9001:1994 have a Δ at the end.

- Is there evidence of planning of production processes?
- Does the planning extend beyond production processes to encompass all product-realization processes? Δ

- Is the planning consistent with other elements of the quality management system? Δ
- Does product-realization documentation exist?
- Are product-realization resources and facilities defined during the planning process and do they appear to be adequate?
- Does the planning define the records that must be prepared to provide confidence of the conformity of the processes and resulting product?

7.2 Customer-related processes

7.2.1 Identification of customer requirements

The organization shall determine customer requirements including:

a) product requirements specified by the customer, including the requirements for availability, delivery and support;

b) product requirements not specified by the customer but necessary for intended or specified use;

c) obligations related to product, including regulatory and legal requirements.

Source: BSR/ISO/ASQ Q9001-2000.

How important to an organization is the process to determine customer requirements? It is so important that it demands attention as a survival issue by virtually every management discipline in the organization. One primary reason why determination of customer requirements is so important is the enormous impact of the quotation and order process on ultimate customer satisfaction; if customer requirements are not bilaterally understood, the probability of achieving ultimate customer satisfaction is seriously diminished. Therefore, it is a business necessity to have an effective process established and implemented to identify customer requirements.

Compliance is not difficult for organizations providing only off-the-shelf catalog products to published specifications or standardized services with normal delivery requirements. However, if customers are purchasing complex systems with custom engineering and/or software to a complex set of commercial terms, it is essential to obtain a clear understanding of customer requirements by whatever means possible, including activities such as holding face-to-face meetings and attending pre-bid meetings.

 Most of the requirements in this clause were included in ISO 9001:1994 (clause 4.3—*Contract Review*), but there is now a specific requirement for the organization to address product requirements that have not been specified by the customer but are necessary for the intended or specified use of the product.

In reality, full determination of customer requirements is often an iterative process. Often there are known issues that may evolve into real requirements at a later stage. In such cases, documentation of the open issues and providing for the attendant business risk is needed and may prove to be an acceptable approach to meeting the requirements of this clause.

 DEFINITIONS

Requirement (2.1.2)—need or expectation that is stated, customarily implied or obligatory

NOTE 1   A qualifier may be used to denote a specific type of requirement, e.g. product requirement, quality system requirement, customer requirement.

NOTE 2   A specified requirement is one which is stated, for example, in a document.

NOTE 3   Requirements may be generated by different interested parties.

Source: BSR/ISO/ASQ Q9000-2000.

CONSIDERATIONS FOR DOCUMENTATION

Determination of customer requirements is a critical activity and generally involves several functions and levels in an organization. It is wise to have a documented procedure to determine all aspects of customer requirements. The procedure should include determining product requirements specified by the customer and product requirements not specified by the customer but necessary for intended or specified use. Also, unique regulatory and/or legal requirements should be considered. This procedure could be included in a broader procedure addressing customer communications (see clause 7.2.3).

Clause 7.2 also does not require any specific quality records. The planning for realization processes covered in clause 7.1 should define the records the organization will keep during the process of determining customer requirements. Organizations should consider keeping the written requirements and any documentation of conversations in which orally transmitted requirements are discussed.

 TYPICAL AUDIT ITEMS FOR COMPLIANCE

Items representing a difference from ISO 9001:1994 have a Δ at the end.

- Does the organization determine customer requirements?
- Does the process include determination of requirements needed but not specified? Δ
- Are records available that provide evidence that customer requirements have been determined?

7.2.2 Review of product requirements

The organization shall review the identified customer requirements together with additional requirements determined by the organization.

This review shall be conducted prior to the commitment to supply a product to the customer (e.g. submission of a tender, acceptance of a contract or order) and shall ensure that:

a) product requirements are defined;

b) where the customer provides no documented statement of requirement, the customer requirements are confirmed before acceptance;

c) contract or order requirements differing from those previously expressed (e.g. in a tender or quotation) are resolved;

d) the organization has the ability to meet defined requirements.

The results of the review and subsequent follow-up actions shall be recorded (see 5.5.7).

Where product requirements are changed, the organization shall ensure that relevant documentation is amended.

The organization shall ensure that relevant personnel are made aware of the changed requirements.

Source: BSR/ISO/ASQ Q9001-2000.

Like clause 7.2.1, this clause applies to all product types, to all market sectors, and to organizations of all sizes. This clause contains similar requirements to clause 4.3.2 in ISO 9001:1994.

The acceptance of an order or the submission of a quote or a tender by an organization creates an obligation on the organization to meet the conditions stated in the order or to provide the goods and services included in the scope of the quotation or tender. The obligation assumed by the organization includes not only the products defined but also ancillary items such as conformance to stated delivery dates, adherence to referenced external standards, and compliance with the commercial terms and conditions applicable to the order, contract, quote, or tender.

The complexity of the order/quote review process is highly dependent on the business of the organization. A process for reviewing verbal orders for off-the-shelf products with 24-hour delivery (for example, software packages) will differ considerably from a process for reviewing a large order for a one-of-a-kind product with a two-year delivery (for example, an order for a control system for an electric power generating station). The review process must also accommodate, as applicable, electronic orders, blanket orders with periodic releases, unsolicited orders, orders through distributors or representatives, faxed orders, and an almost infinite combination of these as well as other possibilities.

With such a spectrum of possibilities, what is an organization expected to do to conform to the requirements? The first step should be to develop a clear understanding of the nature of the various kinds of customer requirements. If, for example, an organization publishes a catalog and accepts only written orders for catalog-listed items to standard delivery times, then a quotation and order or contract-review procedure can be as simple as a one-paragraph statement that a designated individual (for example, a manager, a clerk, or a president) shall review the written order and initial and date the order, indicating that it can be fulfilled. If an organization must cover possibilities that only occur rarely, the organization could simply note in a procedure that any circumstances different from standard terms and conditions will be addressed via a specific quality plan—which can be generated as the unique occasions arise.

Thus, for a simple order-entry process, there can be a very simple, brief and effective contract-review process. For the large, complex contracts or quotations, the review process may involve many organizational entities such as engineering, manufacturing, legal, finance, and quality assurance. Accordingly, the procedures governing such reviews can be complex and lengthy.

A good guideline to keep in mind when developing a process to address the specific requirements of clause 7.2.2 is to balance the risks to the organization with the effort expended in a review of customer requirements, keeping in mind that the purpose of the review is to add value and not to create a bureaucratic morass.

Clause 7.2.2d requires that the organization have the ability to meet requirements. Often with advanced products there is a need to advance the *state of the art* as product development progresses. Such situations should be clearly identified so that the business risks are understood. In such cases, the *defined requirement* can be considered development of the needed technological advance.

When changes to product requirements, orders, contracts, or quotations occur, it is a requirement that the organization assure that relevant documentation is amended and communicated, as appropriate, within the organization.

 CONSIDERATIONS FOR DOCUMENTATION

Organizations should consider documenting a process for review of customer requirements and how these requirements can be met as well as consideration of additional requirements that may be appropriate.

This clause has a specific record requirement that is self-explanatory—keep adequate records of reviews. It is worthwhile to establish minimum retention times for review documents (for example, three years or seven years). Some organizations have a cultural bias to retain such documents forever; however, it is usually not a good idea to create such a requirement by procedure unless required by a contract.

TYPICAL AUDIT ITEMS FOR COMPLIANCE

- Does a process exist to require review of identified customer requirements before commitment to supply a product to the customer?

- Does a process exist to require review of quotes and orders for adequacy of the definition of requirements?

- Is there a procedure for handling review of verbal orders?

- Is there a process documented to handle resolution of differences between quotations and orders?

- Does a process exist for handling changes to product requirements?

- Is objective evidence (that is, records) of quote, tender, contract, and order review available and maintained?

7.2.3 Customer communication

The organization shall identify and implement arrangements for communication with customers relating to:

a) product information;

b) inquiries, contracts or order handling, including amendments;

c) customer feedback, including customer complaints.

Source: BSR/ISO/ASQ Q9001-2000.

   The basic requirements of this clause are not new. Customer communication has always been a requirement. However, the requirements for implementing arrangements with customers for communications on issues such as general feedback or specific complaints are broader in scope and more explicit than the requirements contained in ISO 9001:1994.

The arrangements identified and implemented should be appropriate for the organization in terms of its products, its orders or contracts, and the approaches to be used to obtain customer feedback.

CONSIDERATIONS FOR DOCUMENTATION

Determination of customer requirements is a critical activity and generally involves several functions and levels in an organization. Organizations should consider having a process to assure adequate communications with customers relating to product information, inquiries, contracts, order handling (including amendments), and customer feedback, including customer complaints. The extent to which the process should be documented should be dependent upon the size of the organization and the variety of customer communication links.

TYPICAL AUDIT ITEMS FOR COMPLIANCE

Is there a process in place to communicate with customers relative to product information, inquiries, contracts, order handling (including amendments), and customer feedback including customer complaints?

CHAPTER

6

Design and/or Development

7.3.1 Design and/or development planning

The organization shall plan and control design and/or development of the product.

Design and/or development planning shall determine:

a) stages of design and/or development processes;

b) review, verification and validation activities appropriate to each design and/or development stage;

c) responsibilities and authorities for design and/or development activities.

Interfaces between different groups involved in design and/or development shall be managed to ensure effective communication and clarity of responsibilities.

Planning output shall be updated, as appropriate, as the design and/or development progresses.

Source: BSR/ISO/ASQ Q9001-2000.

The intent of clause 7.3.1 is directed at assuring that the organization plans and controls design and/or development projects. The key reason for this emphasis on planning is to maximize the probability that the project will meet defined customer requirements. If the design and/or development processes are planned and controlled well, an additional benefit will be that projects are completed on time and within budget.

Planning is required to the level of detail necessary to achieve the design objectives—not to generate an excessive amount of paperwork. A typical approach that is used to effectively address the planning requirement is to generate some form of project flowchart that incorporates the pertinent personnel, timing, and interrelationship information. Examples include Gantt charts, PERT charts, or CPM charts. The important effort is the thinking and discussion required to determine how the project will proceed from inception to completion. Stages of the project need to be determined, and responsibilities, authority, and interfaces need to be defined. Requirements need to be established for incorporation of design review, verification, and validation into the design and/or development project. The organization needs to determine how communications will be structured (for example, weekly meetings, periodic reports, or other methods). Use of widely available software can be an effective approach to meeting the planning requirements of the standard.

 DEFINITIONS

Design and development (2.4.7)—set of processes that transforms requirements into specified characteristics and into the specification of the product realization process

NOTE 1   The terms "design" and "development" are sometimes used synonymously and sometimes used to define different stages of the overall design and development process.

NOTE 2   A qualifier may be applied to indicate the nature of what is being designed and developed (e.g. product design and development or process design and development).

Process (2.4.1)—system of activities which uses resources to transform inputs into outputs

Project (2.4.6)—unique process, consisting of a set of coordinated and controlled activities with start and finish dates, undertaken to achieve an objective conforming to specific requirements, including the constraints of time, cost and resources

NOTE 1   An individual project may form part of a larger project structure.

NOTE 2   In some projects the objectives are refined and the product characteristics defined progressively as the project proceeds.

NOTE 3   The outcome of a project may be one or several units of product.

NOTE 4   The organization is temporary and established for the lifetime of the project.

Characteristic (2.5.1)—distinguishing feature

NOTE   There are various classes of characteristic, such as:

physical, e.g. mechanical, electrical, chemical or biological characteristics; sensory, e.g. related to smell, touch, taste, sight, hearing; behavioural, e.g. courtesy, honesty, veracity; temporal, e.g. punctuality, reliability, availability; ergonomic, e.g. linguistic or physiological characteristic, or related to human safety; functional, e.g. range of a plane.

System (2.2.1)—set of interrelated or interacting elements

Source: BSR/ISO/ASQ Q9000-2000.

CONSIDERATIONS FOR DOCUMENTATION

Considerations should include a procedure that states the expectations for formal project plans, including the minimum level of detail for each project. The planning and documentation requirements are frequently a function of the size of the project. Note that the clause requires that the planning be updated as the development progresses. This clause also does not require any specific quality records. Organizations should determine which design and/or development planning records should be retained.

TYPICAL AUDIT ITEMS FOR COMPLIANCE

- Are the stages of the design and/or development project defined? Where?
- Are verification and validation addressed? Are these activities appropriate?
- Is it clear who is responsible for what?
- Are the communications channels defined? Is there evidence that communications on projects is occurring and that it is effective?

7.3.2 Design and/or development inputs

Inputs relating to product requirements shall be defined and documented. These shall include:

a) functional and performance requirements;

b) applicable regulatory and legal requirements;

c) applicable information derived from previous similar designs; and

d) any other requirements essential for design and/or development.

These inputs shall be reviewed for adequacy. Incomplete, ambiguous or conflicting requirements shall be resolved.

Source: BSR/ISO/ASQ Q9001-2000 (with errata).

One of the often quoted, if ludicrous, criticisms of ISO 9001 is that it can be used to assure that a process is in place to produce conforming concrete life preservers. Whoever proffered this criticism did not understand the meaning of clause 7.3.2 (or its equivalent in ISO 9001:1994). It is intended to assure the development and documentation of a requirements specification or an equivalent statement of the general and specific characteristics of a product to be developed, including the suitability of the product to meet marketplace and customer needs.

There are many areas to consider when defining product requirements. Examples include statutory or regulatory requirements (environmental considerations such as ISO 14000 should also be considered); industry standards; national and international standards; organizational standards; safety regulations; customer wants and needs; cost; past experiences; and for designs that are related to specific customer orders, contract commitments.

The result of the consideration of such items is the doc-umentation of a complete and unambiguous statement of product requirements, sometimes called a *requirements specification*. Development work should not begin until such a document exists in a form acceptable to all who have responsibility for contributing to the product specification (at least to the individuals who must bring the product to the marketplace as well as to those who will do the design and/or development). Concurrence with the requirements document by all parties is not required explicitly by clause 7.3.1, but it should be considered to avoid misunderstand-ings during project implementation. It is particularly worth-while to obtain closure, where appropriate, between mar-keting and/or sales and the organizational entity that will be doing the development work. A requirements specification signed by the involved parties is one way to assure that con-cerned parties in an organization are in agreement regarding the product requirements. Such a document can provide the objective evidence of compliance with the requirements of this clause.

 DEFINITIONS

Product (2.4.2)—result of a process

NOTE   There are four agreed generic product categories:
-hardware (e.g. engine mechanical part);
-software (e.g. computer program);
-services (e.g. transport);
-processed materials (e.g. lubricant).

Hardware and processed materials are generally tangible products, while software or services are generally intangible.

Most products comprise elements belonging to different generic product categories. Whether the product is then called hardware, processed mate-rial, software, or service depends on the dominant element.

EXAMPLES   The offered product "car" consists of hardware (e.g. the tyres), processed materials (e.g. fuel, cooling liquid), software (e.g. engine control software, the driver's manual), and service (e.g. the payment facil-ities or the guaranty).

Requirement (2.1.2)—need or expectation that is stated, customarily implied or obligatory

NOTE 1   A qualifier may be used to denote a specific type of requirement, e.g. product requirement, quality system requirement, customer requirement.
NOTE 2   A specified requirement is one which is stated, for example, in a document.
NOTE 3   Requirements may be generated by different interested parties.

Source: BSR/ISO/ASQ Q9000-2000.

CONSIDERATIONS FOR DOCUMENTATION

Design inputs must be documented. Later the design outputs must be documented in a manner that permits verification against these inputs. This means careful thought should be given to the methods for documenting design inputs. Considerations should include:

- Creating a procedure that defines what will be documented to assure product requirements are adequately defined and who will participate in the definition of product requirements
- Creating a procedure that defines the process for review of product requirements for completeness and adequacy

This clause does not require any specific quality records. The planning for realization processes covered in clause 7.1 should define the records the organization will keep during the process of developing the design inputs.

TYPICAL AUDIT ITEMS FOR COMPLIANCE

- Are requirements for new products defined and documented?
- Are the requirements complete?
- Are the requirements unambiguous?
- Are the requirements without conflict?

7.3.3 Design and/or development outputs

The outputs of the design and/or development process shall be documented in a manner that enables verification against the design and/or development inputs.

Design and/or development output shall:

a) meet the design and/or development input requirements;

b) provide appropriate information for production and service operations (see 7.5);

c) contain or reference product acceptance criteria;

d) define the characteristics of the product that are essential to its safe and proper use.

Design and/or development output documents shall be approved prior to release.

Source: BSR/ISO/ASQ Q9001-2000.

This provision of the standard requires the availability of objective evidence that the design and/or development has been executed in accordance with the requirements that were defined at the inception of the project. The objective evidence can be in the form of development reports that contain data to show that the requirements have been satisfied, test results, or any other formal documentation of the results of the effort to develop a product with the specified characteristics.

The conventional documentation of the results of a design and/or development project demonstrate that the product will do what it is expected to do. A more difficult issue to address regarding design output is to document that the product will not do what it should not do. It is especially important, for example, to assure that a software product will not interfere with the operation of other software modules in a computer-based system.

The documentation of the results of a development project is typically the responsibility of the team or individual that performed the work on the project.

In addition to documenting that the output results meet the input requirements, the standard requires that information be provided to facilitate product realization. For hardware products this means that the design team or individual should provide appropriate information to facilitate the production of the product to specified requirements. For software products it is generally not necessary or pertinent to address item 7.3.3b—"provide appropriate information for production and service operations (see 7.5)." For service products, however, it may be necessary to provide guidance to individuals in the organization who are responsible for producing collateral material that will be used in the delivery of the service (for example, training manuals).

Item 7.3.3c requires a clear and unambiguous statement of the requirements that a product must meet in order to be acceptable to customers. Such requirements will typically be incorporated into the test/inspection of the product to assure that the product will conform to defined customer needs. Providing clear definition of product acceptance criteria as an output from product design and/or development is essential for hardware, service, processed materials, and software products.

The output from the design and/or development process must "define the characteristics of the product that are essential to its safe and proper use." The output from the design process is expected to include any information that relates to producing and/or using the product safely and properly. Organizations should pay particular attention to this issue. It not only addresses ultimate customer satisfaction with the product or service, but also the existence of objective evidence that the organization considered the safe and proper use of products may be an important component of demonstrating prudent judgment if there are ever liability issues related to the product or service. Conversely, not having such records could be viewed as evidence of a flawed design and/or development process.

Finally, the standard requires that the output from a design and or development project be processed through an approval process before the product is released. This requirement is included to assure that all aspects of the project have been executed in accordance with documented plans and applicable procedures before the product is launched into production or delivered to a customer.

 ## DEFINITIONS

Objective evidence (2.8.1)—data supporting the existence or verity of something

NOTE   Objective evidence may be obtained through observation, measurement, test, or other means.

Source: BSR/ISO/ASQ Q9000-2000.

 ## CONSIDERATIONS FOR DOCUMENTATION

The specific design outputs must be documented, and that documentation must be in a form that can be used for subsequent design verification. Considerations should include defining in a documented procedure the expectations of developers regarding the form and content of the documentation of the results of a design project.

This clause does not require any specific quality records. But quality records in some form should exist to demonstrate compliance.

 ## TYPICAL AUDIT ITEMS FOR COMPLIANCE

- Does documentation of the output of design and/or development projects exist?
- Does it show how design and/or development outputs satisfy input requirements (for example, as stated in a functional requirements specification)?

- Does output provide, as appropriate, information for production operations?
- Are product acceptance criteria clearly stated?
- Are product safety and use characteristics identified?
- Is there an approval process for release of products from the design and/or development process?

7.3.4 Design and/or development review

At suitable stages, systematic reviews of design and/or development shall be conducted to:

a) evaluate the ability to fulfil requirements;

b) identify problems and propose follow-up actions.

Participants in such reviews shall include representatives of functions concerned with the design and/or development stage(s) being reviewed. The results of the reviews and subsequent follow-up actions shall be recorded (see 5.5.7).

Source: BSR/ISO/ASQ Q9001-2000.

Design and/or development review is used to assure timely release of a new product that fully meets the needs of the customers. It can also contribute significantly to reduced cost. The intent of the standard is to involve all appropriate organizational individuals in the development of a new product as early as feasible in order to understand and address life-cycle issues early in the design and/or development process. Design and/or development review is intended to address more than just the question of whether the product will meet specified requirements. Design and/or development review is intended to address the "abilities" associated with a new product project—manufacturability, deliverability, testability, inspectability, shipability, serviceability, repairability, availability, and reliability, as well as issues related to purchase of components and subassemblies and inventory and production planning. The design review is intended to identify issues, to discuss possible resolutions, and to determine appropriate follow-up.

Design and/or development review is equally applicable to hardware, processed materials, software, and service projects. In fact, it is a critical element of the software design and/or development process. When robust design and/or development reviews are held for software projects, including design review of software test plans, development cycles are typically reduced and life-cycle costs are lower.

A primary design-review issue is to assure the design community that design review will not interfere with the creativity and innovation of the designers or slow down the development process. Rather, it is a process step intended to provide confidence that the spectrum of internal and external customer needs has been considered and addressed with the aim of ultimately assuring external customer satisfaction.

The standard does not prescribe the number of design reviews that should be conducted. This should be determined during the design and/or development planning process and should be modified, as appropriate, during the course of a project. Certainly one design review is a minimum unless conditions warrant formally waiving this requirement. It may in certain circumstances be appropriate to waive this requirement, in which case there should be documentation of the reasons and the authority for the waiver, which should be included in the project files.

Design and/or development reviews are required to be documented. The form of the documentation should suit the circumstances but should include documentation of issues and proposed actions at a minimum.

 DEFINITIONS

Review (2.8.6)—activity undertaken to ensure the suitability, adequacy, effectiveness and efficiency of the subject matter to achieve established objectives

EXAMPLE   Management review, design and development review, review of customer requirements, and nonconformity review

Effectiveness (2.2.13)—measure of the extent to which planned activities are realized and planned results achieved

Efficiency (2.2.14)—relationship between the result achieved and the resources used

Software (2.4.4)—intellectual product consisting of information on a support medium

NOTE 1   Software can be in the form of concepts, transactions, or procedures.
NOTE 2   A computer program is an example of software.

Source: BSR/ISO/ASQ Q9000-2000.

 ## CONSIDERATIONS FOR DOCUMENTATION

Considerations should include defining and documenting the process for conducting design reviews, including who calls the reviews, who will attend, requirements for documenting the reviews, and requirements for follow-up on issues raised during reviews.

This clause requires records of design review. The clause has specific reference to clause 5.5.7 of control of the records generated. These records must include the results of the reviews and follow-up actions. Organizations should also consider including a description of what was included in each review and who conducted the review.

 ## TYPICAL AUDIT ITEMS FOR COMPLIANCE

- Are design and/or development reviews being performed?
- Are they indicated in the project-planning documents?
- Who attends?
- Is the attendance appropriate?
- Are results documented?
- Are follow-up actions taken?

7.3.5 Design and/or development verification

Design and/or development verification shall be performed to ensure the output meets the design and/or development inputs. The results of the verification and subsequent follow-up actions shall be recorded (see 5.5.7).

Source: BSR/ISO/ASQ Q9001-2000.

While this requirement is only two sentences long, it generates much misunderstanding. Verification is a distinct activity; it is different than validation. Both verification and validation were explicitly included in ISO 9001 in 1994 primarily to address the design element of the software sector, and both of these requirements have been retained in ISO/DIS 9001:2000.

Verification is a process step that considers the product after the developers are finished. Verification makes a determination, by any reasonable means, that the product does meet the stated requirements. Verification can be done by review and analysis of test data, by making alternative calculations, by additional testing of the product or its components, or by any other means that the organization chooses.

If issues arise during verification activities, they must be documented and follow-up actions need to be identified. Such actions may require rechecking of the output results against the input specifications and requirements and revalidating the product prior to release.

An important point is that the capability of the product to meet specified requirements is verified and that objective evidence exists to demonstrate the basis for this assertion. This requirement applies equally to all product sectors. The service sector should be particularly attentive to conducting thoughtful product verification since the opportunity to address "non-conformity of product" after it is delivered to a customer usually does not exist. Therefore, service, even more so than for hardware or software, must be right the first time to maximize the probability of customer satisfaction.

DEFINITIONS

Verification (2.8.4)—confirmation and provision of objective evidence that specified requirements have been fulfilled

NOTE 1   The term verified is used to designate the corresponding status.

NOTE 2   Confirmation may comprise activities such as performing alternative calculations; comparing a new design with a similar proven design; undertaking tests and demonstrations; reviewing the design-stage documents before release.

NOTE 3   In the field of metrology, refer to VIM.

Service (2.4.3)—intangible product that is the result of at least one activity performed at the interface between the supplier and customer

NOTE   Service may involve, for example: an activity performed on a customer-supplied tangible (e.g. the repair of a car) or intangible (e.g. the preparation of a tax return) product; the delivery of a tangible product (e.g. in the transportation industry); the delivery of an intangible product (e.g. the delivery of knowledge) or the creation of ambience for the customer (e.g. in the hospitality industry).

Source: BSR/ISO/ASQ Q9000-2000.

CONSIDERATIONS FOR DOCUMENTATION

A procedure should be considered for defining the verification process, including the following:

- Who does verification?
- How should results be recorded?
- How should follow-up of verification issues and reverification be managed?

This clause requires records of design verification results and subsequent follow-up actions. There is also specific reference to clause 5.5.7 for control of the records generated.

TYPICAL AUDIT ITEMS FOR COMPLIANCE

- Is a verification process in place?
- Is it effectively implemented?
- Are follow-up actions recorded?

7.3.6 Design and/or development validation

Design and/or development validation shall be performed to confirm that resulting product is capable of meeting the requirements for the intended use. Wherever applicable, validation shall be completed prior to the delivery or implementation of the product. Where it is impractical to perform full validation prior to delivery or implementation, partial validation shall be performed to the extent applicable.

The results of the validation and subsequent follow-up actions shall be recorded (see 5.5.7).

Source: BSR/ISO/ASQ Q9001-2000.

The difference between validation and verification of design and/or development output has caused much confusion in the past, especially with new users of the standard. As was indicated previously for the verification clause, both verification and validation were explicitly included in ISO 9001 in 1994 primarily to address the design element of the software sector, and both of these requirements have been retained in ISO/DIS 9001:2000.

Design and/or development validation is intended to assure that the design and/or development output conforms to defined user needs and "is capable of meeting the requirements for the intended use." Design and/or development validation is usually performed after successful design and/or development verification. It is worthwhile to state again the difference between verification and validation. In simple language, verification addresses conformance to requirements, while validation addresses meeting defined user needs.

For hardware if a water heater design meets all specified requirements but is not able to be easily installed by a plumber, it would "meet" the intent and requirement of the verification clause but *not* of the validation clause.

For software if the output from a project to design a unit or module of a software product (for example, an SPC package) performed as specified in the SPC requirements specification but caused a word processor to crash when the SPC product was loaded into a system, then this product would "meet" the intent and requirement of the verification clause but *not* of the validation clause.

For service the primary service requirements might be met but secondary factors can suddenly overshadow them. Validation helps to uncover incomplete service requirements. For example, an express mail service that guarantees overnight delivery might meet the schedule, but it is inadequate if the package can be left in a doorway during inclement weather and the package is destroyed by rain. This service would meet the intent and requirement of the verification clause but *not* of the validation clause.

Validation is a particularly important requirement and concept to understand and to address in the world of software product development because of the often mysterious interactions that occur deep in the workings of a computer. In addition to being an ISO 9001 requirement and even though software designers complain that there is never enough time to perform robust validation, this is not an area to be ignored or given perfunctory treatment.

In addition to the customer-satisfaction implications, robust validation processes are critical to the optimization of the life-cycle costs of software (the majority of which typically occur after product release) and to minimizing product-liability exposure. Thus, validation should receive careful attention, and the results should be recorded and retained as quality records.

From the previous discussion, it is obvious that validation is performed after verification and in an environment that approximates as closely as possible the operating conditions that will exist in actual use. Also, whenever possible it should be performed before product is released for shipment. If it is not possible to perform a complete validation of a hardware, software, or service product before release and/or shipment to customers, then a partial validation should be performed to the extent possible. In addition to customer-satisfaction issues, cost containment is a major reason for performing validation before a product is delivered to a customer. Resolution of issues after shipment can be very expensive.

 DEFINITIONS

Validation (2.8.5)—confirmation and provision of objective evidence that the requirements for a specific intended use or application have been fulfilled

NOTE 1   The term validated is used to designate the corresponding status.
NOTE 2   The use conditions may be real or simulated.

Software (2.4.4)—intellectual product consisting of information on a support medium

NOTE 1   Software can be in the form of concepts, transactions, or procedures.
NOTE 2   A computer program is an example of software.

Source: BSR/ISO/ASQ Q9000-2000.

 CONSIDERATIONS FOR DOCUMENTATION

Considerations should include documenting a process for performing design and/or development validation. Clause 7.3.6 requires records of the validation results and subsequent follow-up actions with specific reference to clause 5.5.7 of control of the records generated.

 TYPICAL AUDIT ITEMS FOR COMPLIANCE

- Is design validation performed to confirm that the product is capable of meeting requirements for intended use?
- Is validation completed prior to delivery when applicable?
- Is partial validation provided in cases where full validation cannot be performed prior to delivery?
- Are the results of design validation documented?

> ## 7.3.7 Control of design and/or development changes
>
> Design and/or development changes shall be identified, documented and controlled. This includes evaluation of the effect of the changes on constituent parts and delivered products. The changes shall be verified and validated, as appropriate, and approved before implementation.
>
> The results of the review of changes and subsequent follow up actions shall be documented (see 5.5.7).
>
> NOTE See ISO 10007 for guidance.

Source: BSR/ISO/ASQ Q9001-2000.

During the course of a design and/or development project, there are usually changes to the requirements defined at the design and/or development input stage. Such changes occur for many reasons, including: 1) omissions that become apparent after design and/or development work starts, 2) errors or inconsistencies in the design or in a specification requirement, 3) changes requested by marketing or by a customer, 4) perceived improvement opportunities, 5) changing regulatory or statutory conditions, 6) issues raised in design review, 7) issues raised during the verification process, and 8) issues raised during the validation process.

Any changes that occur in the design of a product, either during the design process or subsequent to delivery of product to a customer, "shall be identified, documented and controlled." This requirement applies to all product sectors and especially to software, where configuration control both during design and/or development and subsequent to product release is a major issue.

Changes to a product should be considered to be like miniprojects within a project. The reason for this requirement is that any changes, even those perceived as "improvements," can have unforeseen adverse effects on other elements of a product or can result in unanticipated system performance when used in a "real life" environment. Therefore, changes should be exercised through design review, verification, and validation processes.

This clause also now requires evaluation of the effect of changes and follow-up actions, if necessary.

CONSIDERATIONS FOR DOCUMENTATION

Considerations should be given to documenting procedures to assure that design and/or development project changes are communicated to all interested parties to assure the recording of changes, to require adequate document processing and control (see chapter 3), and to assure that appropriate authorization is documented for any changes.

This clause requires documentation of the results of the review of changes and subsequent follow-up. The clause also has a specific reference to clause 5.5.7 of control of the *records* generated. Design and/or development changes must be reflected in the design-output documents. Records must also be kept of the design-change reviews themselves and follow-up actions taken.

TYPICAL AUDIT ITEMS FOR COMPLIANCE

Items representing a difference from ISO 9001:1994 have a Δ at the end.

- Are all design and/or development project changes documented?
- Is there evidence to demonstrate that changes are authorized?
- Do records include the results of review of changes?
- Have changes been communicated to interested parties?
- Do records include follow-up actions related to the review of changes? Δ

CHAPTER

7

Purchasing

> ### 7.4.1 Purchasing control
>
> The organization shall control its purchasing processes to ensure purchased product conforms to requirements. The type and extent of control shall be dependent upon the effect on subsequent realization processes and their output.
>
> The organization shall evaluate and select suppliers based on their ability to supply product in accordance with the organization's requirements. Criteria for selection and periodic evaluation shall be defined. The results of evaluations and follow-up actions shall be recorded (see 5.5.7).

Source: BSR/ISO/ASQ Q9001-2000.

The requirements described in clause 7.4 are similar in intent and content to the requirements contained in clause 4.6 in ISO 9001:1994.

The 2000 standard permits the organization to decide the "type and extent of control" which should be based on the effect of the purchased material on the product realization processes and on the products produced. If purchased material has little impact, then minimal control is needed (for example, a screw that is used inside a non-critical subassembly). Generally speaking, minimal control is required for commodity-type purchased material.

If purchased material has high actual or high potential impact on either the final product or the realization processes, then more robust control is required. If, for example, the bolt mentioned previously is used for an aircraft engine mount, then the controls will be more extensive than if the bolt is used in a noncritical application inside a subassembly. Determining the nature of the control is the responsibility of the organization as it considers customer, regulatory, industry, and other appropriate requirements. ISO/DIS 9001:2000 requires the organization to think about what makes sense from both a customer and a business perspective.

The standard still requires the organization to evaluate suppliers and to define the criteria used to select and periodically evaluate suppliers. However, the organization has broad flexibility regarding how to do this and focuses on obtaining conforming material rather than maintaining approved-supplier lists. And, as before, results of all evaluations and any required follow-up actions shall be documented and retained as quality records.

 ## DEFINITIONS

Supplier (2.3.6)—organization or person that provides a product

EXAMPLES   Producer, distributor, retailer or vendor of a product, or provider of a service or information.

NOTE 1   A customer can be internal or external to the supplier's organization.

NOTE 2   In a contractual situation a supplier may be called the "contractor".

Source: BSR/ISO/ASQ Q9000-2000.

 ## CONSIDERATIONS FOR DOCUMENTATION

Organizations should consider developing procedures to describe processes for selection and periodic evaluation of suppliers. Also, organizations should carefully consider how they will communicate their processes for controlling purchased material that will affect customer satisfaction. Typically, organizations will document the process to be used in the form of a procedure to assure understanding of requirements and consistent implementation.

Clause 7.4.1 requires records of the results of supplier evaluations and subsequent follow-up actions with specific reference to clause 5.5.7 for control of the records generated. These records would include reports of supplier evaluations, corrective actions requested of suppliers, and the actual corrective actions taken.

TYPICAL AUDIT ITEMS FOR COMPLIANCE

Items representing a difference from ISO 9001:1994 have a Δ at the end.

- Have criteria for selection and periodic evaluation of suppliers been defined? Δ
- Is there a process for selection and evaluation of suppliers?
- Are results of evaluations documented and retained as quality records?

7.4.2 Purchasing information

Purchasing documents shall contain information describing the product to be purchased, including where appropriate:

a) requirements for approval or qualification of product, procedures, processes, equipment, and personnel;

b) quality management system requirements.

The organization shall ensure the adequacy of specified requirements contained in the purchasing documents prior to their release.

Source: BSR/ISO/ASQ Q9001-2000.

The intent of the requirement is essentially unchanged from 1994. The language used is more general, however, to be applicable to all product sectors. It states that purchasing documents (for example, purchase orders) should provide the information necessary to clearly communicate to suppliers what the organization desires to purchase. The requirement indicates the various types of information that may be pertinent and indicates that these items shall be considered as appropriate.

This clause also requires a process to assure that purchasing documents adequately state all of the requirements for the items to be purchased. This can be accomplished by a process as simple as a sign-off of a purchase order or by a more elaborate process that can involve several layers of review and approval, especially for high-value purchased items.

DEFINITIONS

Release (2.6.9)—authorization to proceed to the next stage of a process

NOTE   In English, in the context of computer software, the term release is frequently used to refer to a version of the software itself.

Source: BSR/ISO/ASQ Q9000-2000.

CONSIDERATIONS FOR DOCUMENTATION

Considerations should include development of a procedure that defines what to include in purchasing documents. Organizations should also consider the need for a procedure that defines an approval process for review and approval of purchasing documents before release to suppliers. Clause 7.4.2 also does not require any specific quality records. The planning for realization processes covered in clause 7.1 should define the records the organization will keep. Consider keeping records of the purchased-material document review and copies of the purchase documents themselves.

TYPICAL AUDIT ITEMS FOR COMPLIANCE

- Do purchasing documents adequately describe the products being ordered?
- Do purchasing documents include, where appropriate, requirements for approval or qualification of product, procedures, processes, equipment, and personnel?
- Do purchasing documents include, where applicable, quality management system requirements?
- Are purchasing documents reviewed/approved to assure they contain adequate description of the specified requirements prior to release?

> ### 7.4.3 Verification of purchased product
>
> The organization shall identify and implement the activities necessary for verification of purchased product.
>
> Where the organization or its customer proposes to perform verification activities at the supplier's premises, the organization shall specify the intended verification arrangements and method of product release in the purchasing information.

Source: BSR/ISO/ASQ Q9001-2000.

There are two distinct requirements in clause 7.4.3. The first is a requirement to assure that purchased material conforms to requirements. In ISO 9001:1994 "Receiving inspection and test" of purchased material was addressed in Clause 4.10.2. In the 2000 standard, the requirements are considerably streamlined, and much more discretion and flexibility is provided to the organization to assure the conformance of purchased product. Nevertheless, a process is required that can include approaches such as the following:

- Certifying suppliers (based on demonstrated performance or process capability) and requiring no inspection and/or test
- Conventional incoming inspection using sampling plans
- One hundred percent inspection (or more)
- Verification at the supplier's facility
- Any combination of these or other approaches

Whatever methods are used, the verification activities must be planned and effectively implemented.

It should also be mentioned that verification of purchased product is directed at purchased product that will be incorporated into the products the organization delivers to customers, not the entire spectrum of products purchased by the organization (for example, pencils, rock salt, and so on would be outside the scope of this clause).

Performing verification activities at the supplier's premises is not common for many organizations. If this is the case, however, a simple statement in the quality management system documentation specifying that "this requirement does not apply and if such a situation ever arises the organization shall prepare a unique quality plan to address the situation" will suffice to meet this requirement. If performing verification activities at the supplier's premises is an applicable requirement, then the purchasing documents should describe the procedures to be followed along with the criteria for release of product by the supplier.

 # DEFINITIONS

Verification (2.8.4)—confirmation and provision of objective evidence that specified requirements have been fulfilled

NOTE 1   The term verified is used to designate the corresponding status.
NOTE 2   Confirmation may comprise activities such as:
-performing alternative calculations;
-comparing a new design with a similar proven design;
-undertaking tests and demonstrations;
-reviewing the design-stage documents before release.
NOTE 3   In the field of metrology, refer to VIM.

Source: BSR/ISO/ASQ Q9000-2000.

 # CONSIDERATIONS FOR DOCUMENTATION

Considerations should include the process for identifying and implementing the activities necessary to assure conformance of purchased product. If verification activities are performed at the supplier's premises, consider preparing a procedure covering the process for performing this verification and for release of the product. This clause also does not require any specific quality records. The planning for realization processes covered in clause 7.1 should define the records the organization will keep. Consideration should be given to keeping records of product verification and product release.

TYPICAL AUDIT ITEMS FOR COMPLIANCE

- Has the organization defined a process for verifying that purchased product conforms to defined requirements?
- Is the process effectively implemented?
- Does objective evidence exist of product acceptance?
- Is verification of purchased product performed at the supplier's premises? If so, are the arrangements specified and does objective evidence exist of effective implementation?

CHAPTER

8

Production and Service Operations

7.5 Production and service operations

7.5.1 Operations control

The organization shall control production and service operations through:

a) the availability of information that specifies the characteristics of the product;

b) where necessary, the availability of work instructions;

c) the use and maintenance of suitable equipment for production and service operations;

d) the availability and use of measuring and monitoring devices;

e) the implementation of monitoring activities;

f) the implementation of defined processes for release, delivery and applicable post-delivery activities.

Source: BSR/ISO/ASQ Q9001-2000.

The total set of requirements pertaining to *Production and service operations* is not significantly different from the requirements of the 1994 standard. This clause appears to contain fewer requirements than the corresponding clauses of the previous standard because all of the requirements for production and service operations are not listed in clause 7.5. Instead, common requirements are now stated only once and are not repeated throughout the standard in order to eliminate redundancy and to simplify the presentation of requirements. This is particularly evident in clause 7.5.1, *Operations control,* which encompasses the requirements from four clauses of ISO 9001:1994 (clause 4.9, clause 4.10, clause 4.12, and clause 4.19).

Documentation requirements for the overall quality management system are stated in clause 4 and do not need to be repeated here. Likewise, clause 7.1 addresses the planning of product realization processes and requires that they be documented in a manner suitable for the organization's method of operation. Process and product-measurement requirements are stated in clause 8.2.3 and clause 8.2.4. ISO/DIS 9001:2000 emphasizes the process approach for the entire quality management system. There is a clear need to view the entire interconnected quality management system, not a collection of individual, stand-alone elements.

The requirements are expressed in more general terms that provide greater clarity as to their meaning for software and service providers. Although these appear in a more general format, they should not be interpreted as lessened or weakened requirements for hardware producers or providers of processed materials.

The focus of clause 7.5.1, *Operations control,* is on the key concept that processes need to be carried out under controlled conditions. Considerations for achieving controlled conditions are presented. The requirements to determine the extent to which production and service operations are planned, established, documented, verified, and validated is presented in clause 7.1. Since clause 7.1 applies to all of the realization processes, these planning and development requirements are not repeated.

The organization should control process operations by considering a number of factors. This begins with understanding the specifications of the product that the processes need to produce or realize. The organization must determine the production and service processes that need to be controlled and the outputs that must be achieved at each stage of processing.

Also, the specific items of equipment that are needed to achieve the product specifications, including their sequence and operating conditions, need to be addressed.

The organization needs to determine the criteria of acceptability for these processes and needs to perform evaluations against these criteria in order to determine suitability (see clause 7.1). One approach is to perform capability studies to demonstrate process suitability. From the determination of suitability, decisions can be made if additional process-development effort is required to achieve the product specifications. Appropriate criteria and controls for these processes need to be determined and implemented to maintain process capability and to prevent nonconformities from occurring. The corresponding work instructions and the associated measurement equipment can be identified. In determining the extent of documentation needed, the organization should consider the criticality of the product, training level of its people, and complexity as well as size of the organization. Controls often include direct measurement of process parameters and characteristics. There may be inspection or test of the output of the process (for example, the product and/or service). In some cases, both may be used. Whichever combination of approaches is adopted, verification activities should be integrated to maximize both the efficiency of the verification and confidence in the resultant product. Overall, this clause requires organizations to think about their operations.

SERVICES

Every service organization should be aware of the necessary requirements and conditions for the proper operation of its planned and offered services and should establish these in writing. One approach is to rank the offered services in the order of their importance, cost, and criticality. It is the task of the organization to plan, monitor, and systematically supervise the fulfillment of services so that the quality objectives can be achieved. For some types of services, there is little or no process equipment to control, as the service consists of actions performed by the service personnel directly for or with the customer. In these cases, the requirements of this clause apply directly to the service personnel and to the processes that control their competence.

As appropriate, release methods need to be developed and implemented prior to providing the service to the customer. The release methods differ in form, timing, and application. For example, airline pilots utilize preflight checklists to verify the fulfillment of requirements prior to flight. It is different in form, timing, and application when an automobile-repair facility uses both test instruments and a vehicle test drive to verify the satisfactory completion of its service prior to releasing a repaired vehicle to the customer. Also, customer-contact employees can receive immediate feedback by asking customers if the services have been adequately provided.

HARDWARE AND PROCESSED MATERIALS

Raw materials, parts, and subassemblies should conform to appropriate specifications before being introduced into processing. However, in determining the amount of test and/or inspection necessary, consideration should be given to the cost of the evaluation activity at various processing stages versus the added value of subsequent activities. The economic impact of discarding or reworking product should be considered when planning material control. In-process materials should be appropriately stored, segregated, handled, and protected to maintain their suitability. Special consideration should be given to shelf life and the potential for deterioration. Where in-plant traceability of material is important to quality, appropriate identification should be maintained throughout processing to ensure traceability to original material identification and quality status. Where important to quality characteristics, auxiliary materials and utilities such as water, compressed air, electric power, and chemicals used for processing should be controlled and verified periodically to ensure uniformity of effect on the process. Where a processing environment (such as temperature, humidity, and cleanliness) is important to product and/or service quality, appropriate limits should be specified, controlled, and verified.

SOFTWARE

Creation of software code usually is part of the design and development process. Mass production of software is a much less daunting task of replicating the code. Nevertheless, it is essential to control the final stages of development through to code replication and subsequent installation and servicing processes.

In this area, configuration management is of paramount importance. The process controls should include procedures for configuration management to the extent appropriate. This discipline should have been initiated early in the design phase and should continue through the life cycle of the software. It assists in the operation and control of design, development, provision, and use of the software and gives the organization visibility into the state of the software during its life. Configuration management can include configuration identification, configuration control, configuration status accounting, and configuration audit.

 DEFINITIONS

Capability (2.1.7)—ability of an organization, system or process to realize a product that fulfills the requirement for that product

Characteristic (2.5.1)—distinguishing feature

NOTE   There are various classes of characteristic, such as:

-physical, e.g. mechanical, electrical, chemical or biological characteristics;

-sensory, e.g. related to smell, touch, taste, sight, hearing;

-behavioural, e.g. courtesy, honesty, veracity;

-temporal, e.g. punctuality, reliability, availability;

-ergonomic, e.g. linguistic or physiological characteristic, or related to human safety;

-functional, e.g. range of a plane.

Process (2.4.1)—system of activities which uses resources to transform inputs into outputs

NOTE 1   Inputs to a process are typically outputs of other processes.

NOTE 2   Processes in an organization typically are planned and carried out under controlled conditions to add value.

NOTE 3   A process where the conformity of the resulting product cannot be readily or economically verified is frequently referred to as a "special process".

Quality characteristic (2.5.2)—inherent characteristic of a product, process or system derived from a requirement

NOTE   A characteristic assigned to a product, process or system (e.g. the price of a product) is not a quality characteristic of that product, process or system.

Release (2.6.9)—authorization to proceed to the next stage of a process

NOTE   In English, in the context of computer software, the term release is frequently used to refer to a version of the software itself.

Requirement (2.1.2)—need or expectation that is stated, customarily implied or obligatory

NOTE 1   A qualifier may be used to denote a specific type of requirement, e.g. product requirement, quality system requirement, customer requirement.
NOTE 2   A specified requirement is one which is stated, for example, in a document.
NOTE 3   Requirements may be generated by different interested parties.

Specification (2.7.2)—document stating requirements

NOTE A specification may be related to activities (e.g. process specification and test specification), or products (e.g. a product specification, performance specification and drawing).

Verification (2.8.4)—confirmation and provision of objective evidence that specified requirements have been fulfilled

NOTE 1   The term verified is used to designate the corresponding status.
NOTE 2   Confirmation may comprise activities such as:
-performing alternative calculations;
-comparing a new design with a similar proven design;
-undertaking tests and demonstrations;
-reviewing the design-stage documents before release.
NOTE 3   In the field of metrology, refer to VIM.

Work environment (2.3.4)—set of conditions under which a person operates

NOTE   Conditions include physical, social, psychological and environmental factors (such as temperature, recognition schemes, ergonomics and polluted atmospheres).

Source: BSR/ISO/ASQ Q9000-2000.

CONSIDERATIONS FOR DOCUMENTATION

There is a specific requirement for implementation of a defined process for release, delivery, and applicable post-delivery activities. An easy way of defining such processes is through the use of procedures. Considerations should include the development and documentation of needed procedures and work instructions.

 TYPICAL AUDIT ITEMS FOR COMPLIANCE

- Are specifications available that define quality characteristic requirements of the product and/or service?
- Has the organization determined the criteria of acceptability for demonstrating the suitability of equipment for production and service operations to meet product and/or service specifications?
- Has the organization demonstrated the suitability of equipment for production and service operations to meet product and/or service specifications?
- Has the organization defined all production and service operations that require control, including those that need ongoing monitoring, work instructions, and/or special controls?
- Are work instructions available and adequate to permit control of the appropriate operations so as to ensure conformity of the product and/or service?
- Have the requirements for the work environment necessary to ensure the conformity of the product and/or service been defined and are these work environment requirements being met?
- Is suitable measuring and monitoring equipment available when and where necessary to ensure conformity of the product and/or service?
- Have monitoring and verification activities been planned and are they carried out as required?
- For hardware, processed material, and software, have suitable processes been implemented for release of the product and for its delivery to the customer?

- Have suitable release mechanisms been put in place to ensure service conforms to requirements?

7.5.2 Identification and traceability

The organization shall identify, where appropriate, the product by suitable means throughout production and service operations.

The organization shall identify the status of the product with respect to measurement and monitoring requirements.

The organization shall control and record the unique identification of the product, where traceability is a requirement (see 5.5.7).

Source: BSR/ISO/ASQ Q9001-2000.

Requirements in this clause are equivalent to those in the 1994 standard. The identification requirements that were in the clause for inspection and test status (clause 4.12 in ISO 9001:1994), have now been combined with this product identification and traceability clause. The standard has been rearranged to present an integrated system and to minimize redundant text. As noted for this entire section, documentation requirements are now contained in clause 4.

Identification and traceability are separate but related issues. The degree of product identification that is needed must be determined, including any requirements for tracking purchased components, materials, and supplies that are uniquely related to the product. Appropriateness depends upon the nature of the product, the nature and complexity of the process, industry practice, and whether identification is required in a contract. Integral to product identification is its status in fulfilling requirements at various stages of production or service development, storage, and delivery as indicated by passing tests and inspections.

In order to be able to trace a product, the product and its component parts must first be identified in adequate detail. Thus, traceability is closely related to identification. Full traceability involves the ability to trace the history, application, or location of an item or activity. This is usually required when there is a need to trace a problem back to its source and when it is necessary to be able to isolate all parts of an affected batch. Records needed to ensure traceability should be defined. For example, traceability is typically a contract requirement for certain medical devices and for defense/space vehicle assemblies.

SERVICES

It may be important to identify specific personnel involved in each phase of a service delivery process. Different personnel may be involved in successive service functions, each of which is to be traceable. For example, the recording through signatures on serially numbered documents in banking operations is often required. In this case, there is no tangible product, but each individual's identification needs to be traceable to provide the appropriate documentation trail. In a different application, signatures often serve as indications of processing status and approval to proceed with payment of, for example, an invoice.

HARDWARE AND PROCESSED MATERIALS

Product identification is often achieved by marking or tagging a product or its container. When the product is visually identical but the functional characteristics are different, different markings or colors may be used. More often quantities of product are segregated into batches with unique batch numbers. Batch definition may be determined by identifying potential sources of batch-to-batch variation. Sources of variation traditionally are the five M's of man (operator), method (or procedure), material, measurement (measurement method and instrument), and machine (or processing step). New batches may be defined as these potential sources change. It is more common, however, to simply use a specific time period and date of production as the batch definition. This requires separate identifiers to be recorded for changes in operators, materials, machine setups, or other factors that impact the batch in order to provide traceability.

SOFTWARE

Software configuration management practices require that each version of a configuration item be identified by some appropriate means. Likewise, there is a need to maintain the status of the verification steps and tests that have been completed. The results achieved by the product or product components at each phase of the development cycle must also be maintained.

 DEFINITIONS

Traceability (2.5.4)—ability to trace the history, application or location of that which is under consideration

NOTE 1   When considering hardware, traceability may relate to:
-the origin of materials and parts;
-the processing history;
-the distribution and location of the product after delivery.
NOTE 2   Traceability may be used in the context of a service, for example, in order to track the degree of completion of the service.
NOTE 3   Cf. definition of traceability in metrology.

Source: BSR/ISO/ASQ Q9000-2000.

 CONSIDERATIONS FOR DOCUMENTATION

Considerations should include a procedure for maintaining identification and for control of product status. Where there are specific requirements for unique identity, the organization should consider preparing a procedure to describe how this is accomplished and recorded. This clause requires records of unique identification in cases where traceability is required.

TYPICAL AUDIT ITEMS FOR COMPLIANCE

- Has the product been identified by suitable means throughout production and service operations?
- Has the status of the product been identified at suitable stages with respect to measurement and monitoring requirements?
- Is traceability a requirement?
- Where traceability is a requirement, is the unique identification of the product recorded and controlled?

7.5.3 Customer property

The organization shall exercise care with customer property while it is under the organization's control or being used by the organization. The organization shall identify, verify, protect and maintain customer property provided for use or incorporation into the product. Occurrence of any customer property that is lost, damaged or otherwise found to be unsuitable for use shall be recorded and reported to the customer.

NOTE Customer property may include intellectual property (e.g. information provided in confidence).

Source: BSR/ISO/ASQ Q9001-2000.

Customer property is product owned by the customer and furnished to the organization for use in meeting the requirements of the agreement between the two. Upon receipt of the product from the customer, the organization agrees to safeguard the product while it is in the organization's possession.

There are no significant differences in requirements with the previous standard. There is clarification that the requirements for control of customer property include all property provided by the customer, including such items as tooling, information, test software, and shipping containers.

One requirement from the 1994 standard that appears to have been dropped is the requirement that the customer must provide acceptable product. Of course, this is still necessary for certain instances, but this can be confusing. It was agreed that this requirement does not belong in the standard. It is part of the relationship and agreement between the organization and customer and, if needed, is better defined in contractual documents. It is fundamental that the customer will provide product that is acceptable for the purpose provided. However, if this is product that needs to be repaired, for example, it would need to be acceptable for repair. If not, the organization might return the product to the customer as not repairable. A contractual business relationship, written or understood, should deal with this situation.

The note makes it clear that information or other intellectual property is a type of customer property.

SERVICES

In many instances this requirement entails a service provided by the organization to the customer. Repair of a piece of equipment requires clearly defining the responsibilities of both parties. An automotive repair shop must not damage a customer's car. On a much larger scale, shipowners contract for repair of ships with private shipbuilders using owner-furnished equipment and owner-furnished material for a ship that often is to arrive at some future date. Equipment and material may be held in inventory before and after repairs are completed by the private shipbuilder. Storage and handling of supplied material must be considered.

HARDWARE AND PROCESSED MATERIALS

Upon receipt of a product, the organization should examine it to check for identity, quantity, and damage. The product should be safeguarded and maintained. The organization may need to provide maintenance or utilize a maintenance contract with a third party. In such instances, the contractual agreements need to be clear as to responsibility.

SOFTWARE

This clause can be a significant factor in operations dealing with software. An example is the case where a customer provides source code to a contract programming organization for modification to incorporate additional features. The organization must exercise care in protecting the original functionality of the software. Detailed agreements typically define these relationships, including verification and validation requirements of the changes.

 ## DEFINITIONS

Verification (2.8.4)—confirmation and provision of objective evidence that specified requirements have been fulfilled

NOTE 1   The term verified is used to designate the corresponding status.
NOTE 2   Confirmation may comprise activities such as:
-performing alternative calculations;
-comparing a new design with a similar proven design;
-undertaking tests and demonstrations;
-reviewing the design-stage documents before release.
NOTE 3   In the field of metrology, refer to VIM.

Source: BSR/ISO/ASQ Q9000-2000.

 ## CONSIDERATIONS FOR DOCUMENTATION

Whether or not a procedure is needed depends upon the nature of customer property, the control requirements laid out by the customer (if any), and the nature and size of the organization. So, for example, it is not always necessary to have a procedure for the protection of confidential information provided verbally by a customer. Also, if the confidential information is provided in a few documents, it may not be necessary to have documented procedures if the organization is a small consulting organization with a single administrative assistant handling and storing all documents. If, on the other hand, the organization is a large corporation with many people potentially handling the documents, it may be appropriate to have documented procedures defining the control of these documents.

This clause requires records of customer property that is lost, damaged, or found to be unsuitable. There is no specific reference to clause 5.5.7 of control of the records generated. The purpose for recording the loss, damage, or unsuitable condition is to report it to the customer. Organizations would be well advised to keep copies of these reports as controlled quality records.

 ## TYPICAL AUDIT ITEMS FOR COMPLIANCE

- Has the organization identified, verified, protected, and maintained customer property provided for incorporation into the product?
- Does control extend to all customer property including intellectual property?
- Does the organization have records that indicate when customer property has been lost, damaged, or otherwise found to be unsuitable?
- Is there evidence that when customer property has been lost, damaged, or otherwise found to be unsuitable that the customer has been informed?

7.5.4 Preservation of product

The organization shall preserve conformity of product with customer requirements during internal processing and delivery to the intended destination. This shall include identification, handling, packaging, storage and protection.

This shall also apply to the constituent parts of a product.

Source: BSR/ISO/ASQ Q9001-2000.

This clause replaces the 1994 requirements for "Handling, storage, packaging, preservation and delivery." These requirements have not been changed in intent, in scope, or in detail of implementation. For those organizations that have a quality system in place that meets these requirements from the 1994 standard, no changes are necessary. The written requirements in the standard have been significantly simplified in order to be more appropriate for all types of organizations and all types of products. The 1994 requirements were written in language easily understood by organizations producing hardware and processed materials. There were significant comments from service providers about the inappropriateness of the 1994 text for their application.

The organization must safeguard and protect the product during and between all processing steps through to delivery. It should have a system for appropriately identifying, handling, packaging, storing, and delivering the product, including its components.

Marking and labeling should be readable, visually or by machine. Considerations should be given to procedures for segregating batches, stock rotation, and expiration dates. Packaging, containers, wraps, and pallets should be appropriate and durable for protecting the product from damage. Suitable storage facilities that include both physical security and protection from the environment should be provided. It may be necessary to check product periodically to detect deterioration. The organization should provide appropriate handling and transportation equipment such as conveyors, vessels, tanks, pipelines, or vehicles to minimize harm due to handling or due to exposure to the environment. Consideration should be given for maintenance of the transportation and handling equipment.

SERVICES

Some services are primarily storage or delivery services. In these instances, the storage or delivery itself is the product offering. This clause can be viewed as an enhancement to the requirements of subclause 7.5.1. Examples include delivery of packages by air freight, trucking services, and food-delivery services.

 DEFINITIONS

Conformity (2.6.1)—fulfilment of a requirement

NOTE   This definition is consistent with ISO/IEC Guide 2 but differs from it in phrasing to fit into the ISO 9000 concepts.

Source: BSR/ISO/ASQ Q9000-2000.

 CONSIDERATIONS FOR DOCUMENTATION

Considerations should include preparation of work instructions needed to ensure proper handling and preservation of product as appropriate.

 TYPICAL AUDIT ITEMS FOR COMPLIANCE

- Does the organization uniquely identify product during internal processing and delivery?
- Does the organization handle the product during internal processing and delivery so as to preserve conformity to customer requirements?
- Does the organization package the product during internal processing and delivery so as to preserve conformity to customer requirements?
- Does the organization store the product during internal processing and delivery so as to preserve conformity to customer requirements?
- Does the organization protect the product during internal processing and delivery so as to preserve conformity to customer requirements?

7.5.5 Validation of processes

The organization shall validate any production and service processes where the resulting output cannot be verified by subsequent measurement or monitoring. This includes any processes where deficiencies may become apparent only after the product is in use or the service has been delivered.

Validation shall demonstrate the ability of the processes to achieve planned results.

The organization shall define arrangements for validation that shall include the following, as applicable:

a) qualification of processes;

b) qualification of equipment and personnel;

c) use of defined methodologies and procedures;

d) requirements for records;

e) re-validation.

Source: BSR/ISO/ASQ Q9001-2000.

Although text changes have been made to provide added clarity, all of the previous requirements of the 1994 standard remain.

Ultimately, the output of processes should provide finished product that meets the customer requirements. Many finished products do not present any difficulty for verification against end-user requirements through visual inspection, direct measurement of product characteristics, or testing of performance. For processes used to create these products, the extent to which all of the production and service processes require validation is based on practical and economic factors. It is always in the best interest of the organization to actually develop and implement processes that are fully capable of meeting finished-product requirements; by so doing, the organization minimizes or eliminates the creation of defective product requiring reprocessing or discarding. To demonstrate that this has been achieved, organizations often validate all major processes. There is a common expression that it is always less expensive to make the product right the first time. From a practical standpoint, the organization must find the best balance between product verification and process validation.

When the processes are such that the achievement of the product specifications cannot be fully verified by the examination of finished product, either at an earlier stage of production or after finishing, process validation must be performed. Inability to fully verify every unit of product may be due to the nature of the testing (for example, the testing is destructive). When verification cannot be done, the process must be validated. Records of validation need to be established and maintained.

 There is now a requirement for defining the conditions and criteria for revalidation. After being validated, processes need to be maintained in a validated state. If changes are made to the process equipment, the product design, the materials used to produce the product, or to other significant factors such as new personnel, the process often requires revalidation. The organization needs to define the conditions that require a revalidation to be performed. Even if no initiating events occur, common practice often requires revalidation after a minimum period of use. In some industries, revalidation is required if a period of five years has elapsed without an intervening validation. Validation should be carried out at appropriate intervals to ensure reaction to changes in market requirements, regulations, standards, or laws in addition to assuring continued acceptable performance of processes.

SERVICES

Examples of service processes requiring validation include those processes that create financial or legal documents and those that deal with professional advice. Validation includes considering a number of factors such as the need to qualify the processing method, the qualifying of service equipment, and having qualified personnel providing the service.

HARDWARE AND PROCESSED MATERIALS

Examples of typical processes for hardware or processed materials that require validation include welding, soldering, gluing, casting, forging, heat treating, and forming processes. Products with quality characteristics that require certain test and inspection techniques for verification such as x-ray examination, ultrasonics, environmental testing, and mechanical stress tests usually require process validation. Validation includes considering qualification of equipment, personnel, and processes.

SOFTWARE

Generally, software—even the simplest of codes—cannot be fully verified through testing. Expectations are that all software needs to be created by controlled processes following the model described in clause 7.3. The methods and extent of the process validations will differ widely based on the criticality and use of the software. Qualification of personnel, equipment, and software development methodologies and procedures is an important aspect of assuring that software conforms to specified requirements.

 DEFINITIONS

Verification (2.8.4)—confirmation and provision of objective evidence that specified requirements have been fulfilled

NOTE 1   The term verified is used to designate the corresponding status.
NOTE 2   Confirmation may comprise activities such as:
-performing alternative calculations;
-comparing a new design with a similar proven design;
-undertaking tests and demonstrations;
-reviewing the design-stage documents before release.
NOTE 3   In the field of metrology, refer to VIM.

Validation (2.8.5)—confirmation and provision of objective evidence that the requirements for a specific intended use or application have been fulfilled

NOTE 1   The term validated is used to designate the corresponding status.
NOTE 2   The use conditions may be real or simulated.

Source: BSR/ISO/ASQ Q9000-2000.

CONSIDERATIONS FOR DOCUMENTATION

Clause 7.5.5 requires that the organization define the arrangements for validation of processes. Considerations should be given to defining these arrangements in a procedure.

This clause also does not require any specific quality records. The planning for realization processes covered in clause 7.1 should define the records the organization will keep. Clause 7.5.5 requires the organization to define any records that are to be kept as a part of process validation. Organizations should consider keeping records of personnel and equipment qualifications where such qualifications are required.

TYPICAL AUDIT ITEMS FOR COMPLIANCE

Items representing a difference from ISO 9001:1994 have a Δ at the end.

- Has the organization determined which production and/or service processes require validation? Have these processes been validated?

- Has the organization determined which production and/or service processes require qualification? Have these been qualified?

- Has the organization determined what personnel need to be qualified, and has it determined the qualification criteria? Have these personnel been qualified?

- Does the organization use defined methodologies and procedures to validate processes?

- Have the requirements for records of validated processes been defined?

- Are records of validated processes maintained?

- Have the processes requiring revalidation been defined? Δ

- Have processes, as required, been revalidated? Δ

- Does adequate documentation exist to assure process validation is effectively implemented?

7.6 Control of measuring and monitoring devices

The organization shall identify the measurements to be made and the measuring and monitoring devices required to assure conformity of product to specified requirements.

Measuring and monitoring devices shall be used and controlled to ensure that measurement capability is consistent with the measurement requirements.

Where applicable, measuring and monitoring devices shall:

a) be calibrated and adjusted periodically or prior to use, against devices traceable to international or national standards; where no such standards exist, the basis used for calibration shall be recorded;

b) be safeguarded from adjustments that would invalidate the calibration;

c) be protected from damage and deterioration during handling, maintenance and storage;

d) have the results of their calibration recorded (see 5.5.7);

e) have the validity of previous results re-assessed if they are subsequently found to be out of calibration, and corrective action taken.

NOTE See ISO 10012 for guidance.

Software used for measuring and monitoring of specified requirements shall be validated prior to use.

Source: BSR/ISO/ASQ Q9001-2000.

The text from clause 4.11 in ISO 9001:1994 has been reduced and modified. The intent has not been to diminish or increase the level of the requirements. Instead, the change in text is intended to make this section more understandable to providers of software and services.

In order to assure that product meets specifications, measurements must be made. The necessary measurements need to be identified along with any special instruments or measuring and monitoring devices needed for making them. This part of the standard is focused on assuring the quality of the measurements and of the measuring and monitoring devices. If the devices used to make measurements are not accurate, are unstable, are damaged in any way, or are inappropriate for making the measurement, then the product may not meet its requirements. Even worse, the organization will not know this. Measuring and monitoring devices need to be capable, and their use needs to be controlled.

All measuring or monitoring instruments or equipment required to assure conformance of product to requirements fall within the scope of this clause.

For both product and process measurements, statistical methods can be useful for demonstrating conformance to requirements. This is particularly true for fulfilling the requirement that "measuring and monitoring devices shall be used and controlled to ensure that measurement capability is consistent with measurement requirements." To summarize, this requirement encompasses two concepts: the concept of achieving and maintaining a capable measurement system and the concept of achieving and maintaining a stable measurement system. Statistical methods may be useful for obtaining assurance that this requirement is fulfilled.

Measuring and monitoring devices that are required to assure conformity of product need to be controlled. This includes measuring and monitoring devices used during design and development, used for inspection and test of raw materials, used for in-process and final testing, and used for monitoring quality once the product has been released to the customer.

The extent of the control to be exercised for the measuring and monitoring devices is listed in items *a* through *e* of clause 7.6 in ISO/DIS 9001:2000. Although the concept of a measurement system is not specifically addressed in the standard, clause 7.6 provides the framework for the establishment and maintenance of a measurement system. ISO 10012 is recommended as a reference source for general background and guidance for a measurement system and for the management of measuring and monitoring devices.

SOFTWARE

Software used in measuring and monitoring devices must be validated.

 ## DEFINITIONS

Measurement (2.10.1)—set of operations having the object of determining the value of a quantity

Measurement control system (2.10.4)—set of operations necessary to achieve metrological confirmation and continuous control of measurement processes

Measuring equipment (2.10.5)—instrument, measurement standard, reference material and/or auxiliary apparatus necessary to implement a measurement process for carrying out a specified and defined measurement

Measurement process (2.10.2)—set of interrelated resources, activities, and influences related to a measurement

NOTE 1   The resources concerned include measuring equipment and measurement procedures and operators.

NOTE 2   Influences are all factors caused by the environment or procedures which may or may not be controlled or controllable and which add to the variability or the bias of the process.

Source: BSR/ISO/ASQ Q9000-2000.

 ## CONSIDERATIONS FOR DOCUMENTATION

Considerations should include a procedure for control of measuring and monitoring devices, including calibration

requirements. Work instructions should also be prepared for the actual work of performing the calibrations.

This clause requires records of calibration results with specific reference to clause 5.5.7 for control of the records generated.

 TYPICAL AUDIT ITEMS FOR COMPLIANCE

- Has the organization identified the measurements to be made?

- Has the organization identified the measurement and monitoring devices required to assure conformity of product to specified requirements?

- Are measuring and monitoring devices used to ensure measurement capability?

- Are measuring and monitoring devices calibrated and adjusted periodically or prior to use against devices traceable to international or national standards?

- Is the basis used for calibration recorded when traceability to international or national standards cannot be done since no standards exist?

- Are measuring and monitoring devices safeguarded from adjustments that would invalidate the calibration?

- Are measuring and monitoring devices protected from damage and deterioration during handling, maintenance, and storage?

- Do measuring and monitoring devices have the results of their calibration recorded?

- Does the organization have the validity of previous results from measuring and monitoring devices reassessed if they are subsequently found to be out of calibration? Is corrective action taken?

- Is software used for measuring and monitoring of specified requirements validated prior to use?

CHAPTER

9

Measurement

> # 8 Measurement analysis and improvement
>
> ## 8.1 Planning
>
> The organization shall define, plan and implement the measurement and monitoring activities needed to assure conformity and achieve improvement. This shall include the determination of the need for, and use of, applicable methodologies including statistical techniques.

Source: BSR/ISO/ASQ Q9001-2000.

This clause applies to all product types (hardware, software, and services), to all market sectors, and to organizations of all sizes. Although this clause is only two sentences in length, some feel that it is one of the most dramatic clauses in ISO/DIS 9001:2000. The other clause of equal dramatic importance is clause 7.1. These two clauses contain the essential requirements of the process model for an organization to address product realization, continual improvement, and customer satisfaction.

Clause 8.1 requires organizations to think about the processes employed to achieve product realization and to assure that the necessary measurement and monitoring activities are defined, planned, and implemented. It is the responsibility of the organization to decide what it needs to measure/monitor, where to measure/monitor, what analyses should be performed, and how the analysis of the data derived from measurement/monitoring should be used. It is worth repeating that the organization decides the "measurement and monitoring activities needed to assure conformity and to achieve improvement." These decisions are not made by the auditors, consultants, the contents of this book, or via interpretations provided by external agencies (for example, by national bodies); rather, they are made by the organization. Herein lies the challenge of ISO/DIS 9001:2000. The organization must take ownership of measurement/monitoring of its processes to the extent needed to effectively manage the organization.

Regarding the requirement for the determination of the need for and use of applicable methodologies including statistical techniques, the intent of the standard is to clarify the requirements contained in ISO 9001:1994 to the extent that the use of statistical techniques is specifically stated as a requirement. ISO/DIS 9004:2000 provides very useful information to organizations regarding considerations for measuring/monitoring of processes that should be considered when determining the quality management system requirements for measurement and monitoring activities.

 DEFINITIONS

Conformity (2.6.1)—fulfilment of a requirement (2.1.2)

NOTE   This definition is consistent with ISO/IEC Guide 2 but differs from it in phrasing to fit into the ISO 9000 concepts.

Source: BSR/ISO/ASQ Q9000-2000.

 CONSIDERATIONS FOR DOCUMENTATION

No specific documentation is advised or necessary to address the requirements of this clause.

 TYPICAL AUDIT ITEMS FOR COMPLIANCE

- Is objective evidence available to demonstrate that the organization has defined, planned, and implemented the measurement and monitoring activities needed to assure conformity and to achieve improvement?
- Is objective evidence available to demonstrate that the organization has determined the need for and use of applicable methodologies including statistical techniques?

> ## 8.2 Measuring and monitoring
>
> ### 8.2.1 Customer satisfaction
>
> The organization shall monitor information on customer satisfaction and/or dissatisfaction as one of the measurements of performance of the quality management system. The methodologies for obtaining and using this information shall be determined.

Source: BSR/ISO/ASQ Q9001-2000.

 An often-voiced criticism of ISO 9001 was that it focused on paper and procedures (form) rather than on assuring the delivery of products that would address customer satisfaction by meeting customer requirements (function). A primary thrust of ISO/DIS 9001:2000 is to increase the emphasis on customer satisfaction, which is, after all, a primary reason for the existence of most organizations. Increased emphasis on customer satisfaction was explicitly and clearly identified as a marketplace need in the market research that was performed by ISO prior to the development of ISO/DIS 9001:2000.

The approaches that an organization should use to comply with this requirement of the standard are not defined. It is the responsibility of the organization to decide what to measure and monitor. For example, organizations that function in regulated markets may choose to monitor customer reports of product deficiencies. A large automobile manufacturer might measure customer satisfaction as reflected in surveys mailed to new car owners. Services providers may choose to use focus groups to probe both satisfaction and dissatisfaction of customers. Software suppliers could monitor reported bugs from field installations The important point is that the organization decides what to monitor and what methods to use.

A few examples of sources of customer satisfaction and/or dissatisfaction information that could be utilized to meet the requirements of this clause include the following:

- Customer complaints
- Returns
- Warranty information
- Customer-satisfaction studies
- Results from focus group meetings
- Customer tracking studies
- Questionnaires and surveys
- Reports from consumer organizations
- Direct customer communication
- Benchmarking data
- Industry group information
- Trade association information

Although organizations typically have many sources of information regarding customer satisfaction/dissatisfaction available, they are often poorly organized and even more poorly utilized. This requirement of the standard should encourage organizations to better utilize the "gold mine" of information readily available to them.

The organization also must decide the extent to which the processes employed extend beyond conformance to requirements to embrace meeting unstated needs and the expectations of customers. This should include price and delivery considerations. The extent of the processes employed is at the discretion of the organization and should be tied to organizational policies (for example, the quality policy) and objectives (for example, the quality objectives).

The standard takes one additional step regarding the requirements to be addressed in the area of customer satisfaction—the requirement that the methods for obtaining and using the information must be determined. This means that the organization must think about how to gather information and what will be done with the information after it is gathered. Many organizations gather information, some make an effort to understand what the information means, and few actually do something to improve the organization and its processes. The intent of the standard is to encourage organizations to plan what to gather, to gather the information, to analyze and understand it, and to take appropriate action.

DEFINITIONS

Conformity (2.6.1)—fulfilment of a requirement

NOTE   This definition is consistent with ISO/IEC Guide 2 but differs from it in phrasing to fit into the ISO 9000 concepts.

Measurement (2.10.1)—set of operations having the object of determining the value of a quantity

Source: BSR/ISO/ASQ Q9000-2000.

 CONSIDERATIONS FOR DOCUMENTATION

While no specific procedure is needed to address this clause, a group of procedures may be needed to address the requirements for customer-satisfaction measurement. Consideration should be given to documentation of what customer information should be gathered, who should gather it, how often it should be gathered, in what form it should be gathered, who will analyze the information, and what will be done with the results of the analysis.

 TYPICAL AUDIT ITEMS FOR COMPLIANCE

Items representing a difference from ISO 9001:1994 have a Δ at the end.

- Is customer satisfaction and/or customer dissatisfaction information monitored? Δ
- Are methods for gathering and using customer information determined and deployed throughout the organization? Δ

8.2.2 Internal audit

The organization shall conduct periodic internal audits to determine whether the quality management system:

a) conforms to the requirements of this International Standard;

b) has been effectively implemented and maintained.

The organization shall plan the audit program taking into consideration the status and importance of the activities and areas to be audited as well as the results of previous audits. The audit scope, frequency and methodologies shall be defined. Audits shall be conducted by personnel other than those who perform the activity being audited.

A documented procedure shall include the responsibilities and requirements for conducting audits, ensuring their independence, recording results and reporting to management.

Management shall take timely corrective action on deficiencies found during the audit.

Follow-up actions shall include the verification of the implementation of corrective action, and the reporting of verification results.

NOTE See ISO 10011 for guidance.

Source: BSR/ISO/ASQ Q9001-2000.

The requirements of clause 8.2.2 have not changed substantively from the 1994 standard. There have been modest changes to reflect improved practices and to clarify the intent of this clause.

It is now clear that audits are to be carried out periodically. Though this was implied before, it was not clearly stated. A one-time set of audits to comply with ISO 9001 in order to obtain registration is not sufficient. As obvious as this is, some argued that periodic audits were not required in the past. It is now clear that a process is required.

Planning for audits takes into account a number of factors. It is now required that the results of previous audits are among the factors to be considered. In planning for audits, audit scope, frequency, and methodologies must be defined. This detail was not explicit in the earlier standard.

The 1994 standard contained a statement requiring independence of the auditors—that is, "personnel independent of those having direct responsibility for the activity being audited." For some, this created confusion and created a burden as to how to implement internal audits. Some thought that independence required that all auditors needed to be from distant parts of the organization or needed to report to separate senior executives. The clarification is simply that the internal auditors cannot be the individuals who perform the activity being audited.

Internal audit of the quality management system is grouped with clauses for measuring and monitoring customer satisfaction (and/or customer dissatisfaction), and for measuring and monitoring processes and product. The message is clear: Internal auditing is a form of measurement specifically focused on the quality management system.

Even as we recognize internal audit of the quality management system as a form of measurement, it continues to be an essential process to provide confidence in the effective implementation of the quality management system. To better understand the role of internal audit, it is useful to consider its role as complementary to that of two other forms of quality management system evaluation—management review and self-assessment.

When evaluating quality management systems, the following four basic questions should be asked in relation to every process being evaluated:

• Is the process identified and appropriately described?
• Are responsibilities assigned?

- Are required procedures implemented and maintained?
- Is the process effective in achieving the required results?

The collective answers to the above questions determine the outcome of the evaluation.

Evaluation of a quality management system can vary in scope and typically encompasses the following three major approaches:

- Auditing, an aspect of which is the subject of this section, ISO/DIS 9001:2000, clause 8.2.2, *Internal audit*
- Reviewing the quality management system, the subject of ISO/DIS 9001:2000, clause 5.6, *Management review*
- Self-assessments, the subject of ISO/DIS 9004:2000, clause 8.2.1.5, *Self-assessment*

Audits are used to evaluate the adequacy of quality management system documentation, conformance to quality management system requirements and the effectiveness of system implementation. Results of audits can be used to identify opportunities for improvment. There is a slight difference in the way ISO 9001:2000 describes determination of the effectiveness of the quality management system. The 1994 version had auditors determining the system's suitability and effectiveness, the 2000 version requires auditors to determine the effectiveness of implementation. Determination of overall system suitability and effectiveness is left to management using audit results and other data to make that evaluation.

First party audits are conducted by or on behalf of the organization for internal purposes and can form the basis for an organization's self-declaration of conformity. Second-party audits are conducted by customers of the organization or by other persons on behalf of a customer. Third-party audits are conducted by external independent audit service organizations. Such organizations can verify conformity with requirements such as those of ISO 9001.

One role of top management is to carry out regular systematic evaluations of the suitability, adequacy, effectiveness, and efficiency of the quality management system with respect to the quality policy and objectives. This review (see

ISO/DIS 9001:2000, clause 5.6) can include consideration of the need to adapt the quality policy and objectives in response to changing needs and expectations of interested parties. The review includes determination of the need for actions. Among other sources of information, audit reports are used for review of the quality management system.

An organization's self-assessment (see ISO/DIS 9004: 2000, clause 8.2.1.5) is a comprehensive, systematic, and regular review of the organization's activities and results referenced against the quality management system or a model of excellence. The use of self-assessment methodology can provide an overall view of the performance of the organization and the degree of maturity of the quality management system. It can also help to identify areas requiring improvement in the organization and to determine priorities. Such self-assessments are typically not audits to assess conformance to requirements. Rather, they look for opportunities for the organization to improve its efficiency and performance.

Internal quality audits must be conducted periodically and should be used to determine conformity to the requirements of ISO/DIS 9001:2000 and the degree to which the quality management system has been effectively implemented and maintained. An indicator of problems with the effectiveness of the quality management system is the occurrence of high numbers of customer complaints or of high levels of scrap and rework within the organization. As given in clause 8.2.1, organizations are expected to monitor customer satisfaction and/or dissatisfaction. Internal auditors often use this information to identify product-realization processes that require further investigation regarding the extent to which they have been effectively implemented and maintained. In a similar fashion, scrap and rework information may be of value for identifying subject areas for the internal audit.

Whatever factors and methods are used, internal quality audits may be performed on elements of the quality management system or on the entire system. Whatever approach is used, details need to be established in plans and a prioritization should be employed to identify quality system elements requiring investigation. Previous audit results should be among these factors. The scope of each audit should be clear, and the frequency of audits within the audit program and the audit methodology should be identified. Auditors should not have responsibility for the area being audited. This does not preclude persons who have specific functions and responsibilities within the organization from being internal auditors, but they should only audit other functions and other areas within the organization. Internal auditors should be qualified as auditors. This is particularly necessary for "guest" auditors, or technical experts from other functions who are used to provide product or process technical expertise to the effort to evaluate effectiveness but who tend to be inexperienced at auditing.

Audit results should be in a written report, and records should indicate deficiencies. Management should establish target dates for responding to audit findings and should take timely corrective action. Audit results are required to be inputs to management reviews.

Follow-up actions should be evaluated to assure the effectiveness of the corrective actions. This effectiveness should be reported to management.

 ## DEFINITIONS

Management (2.2.6)—coordinated activities to direct and control an organization

NOTE   In English, when the term "management" refers to people, i.e. a person or group of people with authority and responsibility for the conduct and control of an organization, it should not be used without some form of qualifier. For example, "management shall . . ." is deprecated whereas "top management shall . . ." is acceptable.

Procedure (2.4.8)—specified way to carry out an activity or a process

NOTE 1   Procedures may be documented or not.

NOTE 2   When a procedure is documented, the term "written procedure" or "documented procedure" is frequently used.

Corrective action (2.6.5)—action taken to eliminate the cause of a detected nonconformity or other undesirable situation

NOTE 1   Corrective action is taken to prevent recurrence whereas preventive action is taken to prevent occurrence.

NOTE 2   There is a distinction between correction and corrective action.

Record (2.7.6)—document stating results achieved or providing evidence of activities performed

NOTE   Quality records may be used to document traceability and to provide evidence of verification, preventive action and corrective action.

Verification (2.8.4)—confirmation and provision of objective evidence that specified requirements have been fulfilled

NOTE 1   The term verified is used to designate the corresponding status.

NOTE 2   Confirmation may comprise activities such as:

-performing alternative calculations;

-comparing a new design with a similar proven design;

-undertaking tests and demonstrations; reviewing the design-stage documents before release.

Audit (2.9.1)—systematic, independent and documented process for obtaining evidence and evaluating it objectively to determine the extent to which audit criteria are fulfilled

Audit programme (2.9.2)—set of audits to be carried out during a planned time frame

Audit scope (2.9.3)—extent and range of a given audit

NOTE   The scope may be expressed in terms of factors such as physical location, organizational units, activities and processes

Audit criteria (2.9.4)—set of policies, procedures or requirements against which collected audit evidence is compared

Audit evidence (2.9.5)—records, verified statements of fact or other information relevant to the audit

NOTE   Audit evidence can be qualitative or quantitative.

Audit findings (2.9.6)—results of the evaluation of the collected audit evidence against audit criteria

Audit conclusions (2.9.7)—outcome of an audit decided by the audit team after consideration of all the audit findings

Audit client (2.9.8)—person or organization requesting an audit

Auditee (2.9.9)—organization being audited

Audit team (2.9.10)—one or more auditors conducting an audit, one of whom is appointed as leader

NOTE 1   The audit team may also include auditors-in-training and, where required, technical experts.

NOTE 2   Observers may accompany the audit team but do not act as part of it.

Auditor (2.9.11)—person qualified and competent to conduct audits

Technical expert (2.9.12)—<audit> person who provides specific knowledge or expertise with respect to a particular subject field to be audited

Qualification (2.9.13)—<audit> combination of personal attributes, minimum education, training, work and audit experience, and competencies possessed by an auditor.

Source: BSR/ISO/ASQ Q9000-2000.

CONSIDERATIONS FOR DOCUMENTATION

A documented procedure is required that describes the responsibilities and requirements for conducting audits, for ensuring the independence of the audits, for recording results, and for reporting the audit results to management.

This clause also does not require any specific quality records. The planning for realization processes covered in clause 7.1 should define the records the organization will keep. It would usually be expected of the organization to have records of audit plans and descriptions of audits, including their scope, frequency, and methodologies used. Records would be expected to be available that provide evidence that audit findings were reported to management and that there was timely corrective action on deficiencies found during the audit. There should also be records that verification was performed for the implementation of corrective action and that the verification results were reported to management.

TYPICAL AUDIT ITEMS FOR COMPLIANCE

- Does the organization conduct periodic audits of the quality management system?

- Do the periodic audits evaluate the conformity of the quality management system to the requirements of ISO/DIS 9001:2000?

- Do the periodic audits evaluate the degree to which the quality management system has been effectively implemented and maintained?

- Does the organization plan the audit program taking into consideration the status and importance of areas to be audited?

- Does the organization plan the audit program taking into consideration the results of previous audits?

- Are the audit scope, frequency, and methodologies defined?

- Are audits performed by personnel other than those who perform the activity being audited?

- Is there a documented procedure that includes the responsibilities and requirements for conducting audits?

- Is there a documented procedure that describes how to ensure the independence of auditors?

- Is there a documented procedure for recording results and reporting to management?

- Does management take timely corrective action on deficiencies found during the audit?

- Do follow-up actions include the verification of the implementation of corrective action?

- Do follow-up actions include the reporting of verification results?

8.2.3 Measurement and monitoring of processes

The organization shall apply suitable methods for measurement and monitoring of those realization processes necessary to meet customer requirements. These methods shall confirm the continuing ability of each process to satisfy its intended purpose.

Source: BSR/ISO/ASQ Q9001-2000.

Some consider clause 8.2.3 to be a new requirement. In fact, it is not. The different measurement and monitoring activities required for the quality management system are now all listed under ISO/DIS 9001:2000, clause 8.2, *Measurement and monitoring.* Clause 4.9, *Process control,* in ISO 9001:1994 required "monitoring and control of suitable process parameters and product characteristics," which had the same intent as this clause.

The organization needs to define, plan, and implement the measurement and monitoring activities needed to assure conformity and to achieve improvement of the product-realization processes. This requires proactive control of the processes that are used to create product. This clause deals with the measurements that are used to achieve this control.

The key realization processes that have the greatest impact on meeting customer requirements need to be identified. Realistically, not all processes or all process parameters can be measured and monitored. The number of even the most basic of processes and their set of process parameters that are candidates for monitoring can be overwhelming. Clause 8.4, *Analysis of data,* of ISO/DIS 9001:2000 can be a valuable source of information in identifying the key processes and the needed measurements to use for process control. It encompasses the use of applicable methodologies, including statistical techniques. Data from capability studies commonly are used to help determine what processes have high inherent variation and require tight control versus what processes are both capable and relatively stable. This results in a reasonable number of processes and parameters for use in process control.

The requirements for these key realization processes should be quantified either by process parameter specifications or by specifications for the product output of the process. Process-measurement results should be available for the key realization processes. These results should indicate fulfillment of the requirements and should confirm the continuing suitability of each process to satisfy its intended purpose.

 **DEFINITIONS**

Measurement (2.10.1)—set of operations having the object of determining the value of a quantity

Measurement process (2.10.2)—set of interrelated resources, activities, and influences related to a measurement

NOTE 1   The resources concerned include measuring equipment, and measurement procedures and operators.

NOTE 2   Influences are all factors caused by the environment or procedures which may or may not be controlled or controllable and which add to the variability or the bias of the process.

Requirement (2.1.2)—need or expectation that is stated, customarily implied or obligatory

NOTE 1   A qualifier may be used to denote a specific type of requirement, e.g. product requirement, quality system requirement, customer requirement.

NOTE 2   A specified requirement is one which is stated, for example, in a document.

NOTE 3   Requirements may be generated by different interested parties.

Process (2.4.1)—system of activities which uses resources to transform inputs into outputs

NOTE 1   Inputs to a process are typically outputs of other processes.

NOTE 2   Processes in an organization typically are planned and carried out under controlled conditions to add value.

NOTE 3   A process where the conformity of the resulting product cannot be readily or economically verified is frequently referred to as a "special process".

Record (2.7.6)—document stating results achieved or providing evidence of activities performed

NOTE   Quality records may be used to document traceability and to provide evidence of verification, preventive action and corrective action.

Source: BSR/ISO/ASQ Q9000-2000.

 CONSIDERATIONS FOR DOCUMENTATION

Objective evidence confirming the effective operation and control of processes for measuring and monitoring realization processes needs to be available. This will vary depending upon the size and type of organization, complexity and interaction of processes, and competence of personnel. Objective

evidence may be in the form of documented procedures and documented records, particularly where manual measurement processes are used. This may be demonstrated through observation of these measurement and monitoring processes, particularly when online sensors and electromechanical, closed-loop feedback systems are employed.

TYPICAL AUDIT ITEMS FOR COMPLIANCE

- Have the key realization processes necessary to meet customer requirements been identified?
- Are suitable methods employed to measure and monitor these key realization processes?
- Are the intended purposes of the key realization processes quantified by process parameter specifications, by specifications for the product output of the process, or by some other means?
- Are the measurement and monitoring methods for realization processes adequate for confirming the continuing suitability of each process to satisfy its intended purpose?

8.2.4 Measurement and monitoring of product

The organization shall measure and monitor the characteristics of the product to verify that requirements for the product are met. This shall be carried out at appropriate stages of the product realization process.

Evidence of conformity with the acceptance criteria shall be documented. Records shall indicate the authority responsible for release of product (see 5.5.7).

Product release and service delivery shall not proceed until all the specified activities have been satisfactorily completed, unless otherwise approved by the customer.

Source: BSR/ISO/ASQ Q9001-2000.

The requirements of ISO 9001:1994 for measuring and monitoring product have not significantly changed. Like the previous clause on process measurement, some consider this to be a new requirement. In fact, it is not; rather, it is a simplification of ISO 9001:1994, clause 4.10, *Inspection and testing*. The requirements for measuring and monitoring of product, whether they are for software, hardware, processed material or a service, are all now stated in this generic clause. The previous standard was criticized because the text of clause 4.10 was not in generic language. For example, a service provider had tremendous difficulty in understanding what was meant by "release under positive-recall procedures shall not preclude the activities outlined in . . ." (ISO 9001:1994, clause 4.10.3). The generic nature of the current text is not intended to reduce the requirement to measure and monitor the characteristics of the product to verify that requirements for the product are met.

The scope of this clause includes all measurement activities associated with materials, components, assemblies, and product from receiving inspection to product delivery. It covers the actual measurements used to verify that requirements are met for the materials that go into the product as well as the product itself at appropriate stages of the product-realization processes.

For purchased material, clause 7.4.2, *Verification of purchased product,* from ISO/DIS 9001:2000 requires the organization to identify and implement verification activities. Product in this clause of the standard is synonymous with material. The requirements for the associated measures are contained here, in ISO/DIS 9001:2000, clause 8.2.4, *Measurement and monitoring of product.*

For in-process and final product, clause 7.5.1, *Operations control,* from ISO/DIS 9001:2000 requires the organization to implement defined processes for monitoring, release, and delivery.

Conformity to requirements needs to be documented. Records need to indicate who within the organization has the authority to release final product. Analysis of the data for release and also for improvement is detailed in ISO/DIS

9001:2000, clause 8.4, *Analysis of data*. This includes the use of applicable methodologies, including statistical techniques to determine the type of data to collect and the decision rules for release.

Product release and service delivery requires that all specified activities be accomplished unless otherwise approved by the customer. This usually means that some form of record is available to document that specified activities have been accomplished.

 DEFINITIONS

Requirement (2.1.2)—need or expectation that is stated, customarily implied or obligatory

NOTE 1   A qualifier may be used to denote a specific type of requirement, e.g. product requirement, quality system requirement, customer requirement.
NOTE 2   A specified requirement is one which is stated, for example, in a document.
NOTE 3   Requirements may be generated by different interested parties.

Product (2.4.2)—result of a process

NOTE   There are four agreed generic product categories:
-hardware (e.g. engine mechanical part);
-software (e.g. computer program);
-services (e.g. transport);
-processed materials (e.g. lubricant).
Hardware and processed materials are generally tangible products, while software or services are generally intangible.
Most products comprise elements belonging to different generic product categories. Whether the product is then called hardware, processed material, software or service depends on the dominant element.
EXAMPLES   The offered product "car" consists of hardware (e.g. the tires), processed materials (e.g. fuel, cooling liquid), software (e.g. engine control software, the driver's manual), and service (e.g. the payment facilities or the guaranty).

Characteristic (2.5.1)—distinguishing feature

NOTE   There are various classes of characteristic, such as:
-physical, e.g. mechanical, electrical, chemical or biological characteristics;
-sensory, e.g. related to smell, touch, taste, sight, hearing;
-behavioural, e.g. courtesy, honesty, veracity;

-temporal, e.g. punctuality, reliability, availability;

-ergonomic, e.g. linguistic or physiological characteristic, or related to human safety;

-functional, e.g. range of a plane.

Quality characteristic (2.5.2)—inherent characteristic of a product, process or system derived from a requirement

NOTE   A characteristic assigned to a product, process or system (e.g. the price of a product) is not a quality characteristic of that product, process or system.

Conformity (2.6.1)—fulfilment of a requirement

NOTE   This definition is consistent with ISO/IEC Guide 2 but differs from it in phrasing to fit into the ISO 9000 concepts.

Record (2.7.6)—document stating results achieved or providing evidence of activities performed

NOTE   Quality records may be used to document traceability and to provide evidence of verification, preventive action and corrective action.

Measurement (2.10.1)—set of operations having the object of determining the value of a quantity

Measurement process (2.10.2)—set of interrelated resources, activities, and influences related to a measurement

NOTE 1   The resources concerned include measuring equipment, and measurement procedures and operators.

NOTE 2   Influences are all factors caused by the environment or procedures which may or may not be controlled or controllable and which add to the variability or the bias of the process.

Objective evidence (2.8.1)—data supporting the existence or verity of something

NOTE   Objective evidence may be obtained through observation, measurement, test, or other means.

Source: BSR/ISO/ASQ Q9000-2000.

CONSIDERATIONS FOR DOCUMENTATION

Consideration should be given to the work instructions needed to ensure that measurement of product is conducted as planned. Records are required to provide objective evidence that the product acceptance criteria have been met.

They should also indicate the authority responsible for release of the product. This clause contains specific reference to clause 5.5.7 for control of the records generated.

 ## TYPICAL AUDIT ITEMS FOR COMPLIANCE

- Does the organization measure and monitor product characteristics to verify that product requirements are met?
- Does the organization measure and monitor product characteristics at appropriate stages of the product-realization process?
- Is there objective evidence that acceptance criteria for product have been met?
- Is there identification of the authority responsible for release of the product?
- Are all specified activities performed prior to product release and service delivery?
- If there are instances where all specified activities have not been performed prior to product release or service delivery, has the customer been informed and approved of the action?

CHAPTER

10

Control of Nonconformity

8.3 Control of nonconformity

The organization shall ensure that product which does not conform to requirements is identified and controlled to prevent unintended use or delivery. These activities shall be defined in a documented procedure.

Nonconforming product shall be corrected and subject to re-verification after correction to demonstrate conformity.

When nonconforming product is detected after delivery or use has started, the organization shall take appropriate action regarding the consequences of the nonconformity.

It will often be required that the proposed rectification of nonconforming product be reported for concession to the customer, the end-user, regulatory body or other body.

Source: BSR/ISO/ASQ Q9001-2000.

A primary requirement of clause 8.3 is to assure the effective implementation of processes that prevent unintended use or delivery of product that does not conform to requirements. This is a simple requirement that makes business sense. The challenge to an organization is to devise processes to accomplish this objective in a way that encourages personnel to address nonconformity of product rather than to find ways to avoid identification and control of such product.

This clause also requires the organization to take appropriate action when the organization delivers product that is subsequently determined to be nonconforming. Although not explicitly stated, records of such action should be maintained, if only to document the use of prudent judgment in addressing such situations. And finally, when it is required (for example, by contract or by internal procedures) to report a proposed rectification of nonconforming product for concession to the customer, the end user, a regulatory body, or any other body, the organization should have processes in place to assure that such reporting to the customer occurs.

Typically, organizations will establish processes that provide for review of nonconformity by appropriate individuals in the organization. Such processes may have different levels of approval depending on the nature of the decision regarding the action to be taken for the nonconformity. A decision to "use as is," for example, may require engineering approval, while manufacturing management may be permitted to approve a rework or scrap disposition of a nonconformity.

Note that the second paragraph of this clause requires that all nonconforming product be corrected and that when corrections are made, the organization must reverify the product to demonstrate conformity. There are frequently circumstances where organizations will not correct nonconforming product. Products that meet functional requirements are often used "as is," without taking action to make the product fully conform with all requirements, especially if such a decision will not affect the conformance of the end product ultimately delivered to a customer. Also, nonconforming product may be scrapped or regraded, or for purchased material, it may be returned to a supplier. It is expected that the wording of clause 8.3 will be modified in the FDIS to clarify the intent of this clause.

Excluding the issue described above, the content of clause 8.3 is consistent with the requirements contained in ISO 9001:1994. However, the wording is intended to provide broader discretion to the organization in the actual implementation of processes to address nonconformity.

 DEFINITIONS

Conformity (2.6.1)—fulfilment of a requirement (2.1.2)

NOTE   This definition is consistent with ISO/IEC Guide 2 but differs from it in phrasing to fit into the ISO 9000 concepts.

Nonconformity (2.6.2)—nonfulfilment of a requirement (2.1.2)

Correction (2.6.6)—action taken to eliminate a detected non-conformity (2.6.2)

NOTE 1   A correction may or may not be made in conjunction with a corrective action (2.6.5).

NOTE 2   A correction may involve repair (2.6.10), rework (2.6.11) or regrade (2.6.12).

Concession (2.6.8)—authorization to use or release a product (2.4.2) that does not conform to specified requirements (2.1.2)

NOTE   A concession is typically limited to the delivery of a product that has nonconforming characteristics (2.5.1) within specified limits for an agreed time or quantity of product

Release (2.6.9)—authorization to proceed to the next stage of a process (2.4.1)

NOTE   In English, in the context of computer software, the term release is frequently used to refer to a version of the software itself.

Defect (2.6.3)—nonfulfilment of a requirement (2.1.2) related to an intended or specified use

NOTE 1   The distinction between the terms defect and nonconformity (2.6.2) is important as it has legal connotations, particularly those associated with product liability issues. Consequently the term "defect" should be used with extreme caution.

NOTE 2   The intended use may be affected by the nature of the information, such as manuals, provided by the supplier (2.3.6).

Repair (2.6.10)—action taken on a nonconforming product (2.4.2) to make it acceptable for the intended usage

NOTE   Repair includes remedial action taken on a once conforming product to restore it for use, for example, as part of maintenance.

Rework (2.6.11)—action taken on a nonconforming product (2.4.2) to make it conform to the requirements (2.1.2)

Regrade (2.6.12)—alteration of the grade (2.1.4) of a nonconforming product (2.4.2) in order to make it conformant with requirements (2.1.2) differing from the initial ones

Scrap (2.6.13)—action taken on a nonconforming product (2.4.2) to preclude its originally intended usage

EXAMPLES   Recycling, disposal or destruction.

NOTE   In a nonconforming service (2.4.3) situation, usage is precluded by "discontinuance" of the service.

Source: BSR/ISO/ASQ Q9000-2000.

CONSIDERATIONS FOR DOCUMENTATION

A documented procedure is required to ensure that product that does not conform to requirements is identified and controlled to prevent unintended use or delivery. The organization should consider documenting a process for addressing the disposition of nonconforming product and, where appropriate, reverifying the product. This documentation could be a separate procedure or a part of a comprehensive nonconformity procedure.

The organization should also consider documenting a process for addressing situations where nonconforming product is detected after delivery to or use by a customer has occurred. Finally, documenting a process for communication with customers, where appropriate, of circumstances that involve proposed rectification of product nonconformity should be considered. This documentation could be in the form of separate procedures or as a part of a comprehensive nonconformity procedure.

TYPICAL AUDIT ITEMS FOR COMPLIANCE

- Is there a documented procedure to assure that product that does not conform to requirements is identified and controlled to prevent unintended use or delivery?
- Is there evidence of appropriate action being taken when nonconforming product has been detected after delivery or use has started?
- Is it required that any proposed rectification of nonconforming product be reported for concession to the customer, the end-user, or a regulatory body?
- Is there objective evidence of appropriate communication with a customer when the organization proposes rectification of nonconforming product?

CHAPTER
11

Analysis of Data

> ## 8.4 Analysis of data
>
> The organization shall collect and analyse appropriate data to determine the suitability and effectiveness of the quality management system and to identify improvements that can be made. This includes data generated by measuring and monitoring activities and other relevant sources.
>
> The organization shall analyse this data to provide information on:
>
> a) customer satisfaction and/or dissatisfaction;
>
> b) conformance to customer requirements;
>
> c) characteristics of processes, product and their trends;
>
> d) suppliers.

Source: BSR/ISO/ASQ Q9001-2000.

Collection of data without developing the data into useful information is a waste of organizational resources. The purpose of analysis is to convert data into usable information. One of the most important considerations in establishing data-collection methods is to determine how the data will be used. When a data collection scheme has been well designed, the analysis effort is minimized. Data-collection systems that are poorly designed cannot only be inefficient, but they can also yield incorrect information.

In reference to preventive action, clause 4.14.3a of ISO 9001:1994 requires that certain sources of information be used to ". . . detect, analyze, and eliminate potential causes of nonconformities. . . ." With the exception of this clause, ISO 9001:1994 is silent on the concept of analysis.

ISO/DIS 9001:2000 goes beyond the ISO 9001:1994 requirement to use analysis in the preventive action process to eliminate potential causes of nonconformity. It states the following two purposes for analyzing data:

- To determine the suitability and effectiveness of the quality management system
- To identify improvements that can be made to the quality management system

An organization dedicated to continual improvement will view the requirements of clauses 5, 7, and 8 as linked in the sense that the organization should function on a closed-loop basis. This means continually measuring processes and products, analyzing data, and improving the system.

Information from analysis of data should be used as part of the management review input. Analysis may also be conducted as a part of the management review itself. Clause 8.4 requires analysis to determine the suitability and effectiveness of the quality management system, and clause 5.6.1 requires that top management review the quality management system to ensure its suitability, adequacy, and effectiveness. Top management has a good deal of flexibility in complying with these requirements. Options for top management include the following:

- Data may be analyzed "off line," and information from the analysis may be provided as input to top management for use in determining suitability and effectiveness of the system. This may be typical of larger organizations or organizations with dedicated analytical staff.
- The data may be provided to top management; in this case, top managers would conduct the analysis as a part of the management review. This may be more typical for a small organization.

The organization is required to analyze data to identify areas where improvements can be made. The analysis must provide information in four specific areas: customer satisfaction and/or dissatisfaction; conformance to customer requirements; characteristics of processes, product and their trends; and suppliers. The specific information that is appropriate may differ based on the type and size of the organization as well as on the product category.

Customer satisfaction and/or dissatisfaction information is different from the information related to meeting customer requirements. It is possible for customers to be satisfied with product that is nonconforming or to be highly dissatisfied with product that fully conforms with requirements. In either case, identification of the situation offers an opportunity to change requirements to reflect actual customer needs. Measurement of customer information may include such items as issues of importance to customers, gaps in meeting customer expectations, customers' desires for changes in characteristics or features of the product, the relative satisfaction of customers with the organization and its competitors, and/or the organization's most significant customer-complaint areas. The appropriate information on customer satisfaction and/or dissatisfaction may depend upon the nature of an organization's relationships with its customers. For example, large organizations selling products to consumers through multiple distribution channels may need information related to several tiers of customers in their value chain. This may include information on the several distribution channels and on consumers as well. This could be the case for toy manufacturers (hardware), home computer software providers (software), and airlines (service). At another extreme, organizations with a single customer and day-to-day personal customer contact may have significantly different information needs.

Information related to conformance to customer requirements is information that describes how well the customer's requirements are being met. It includes information on those requirements the organization has derived from needs and expectations not specifically stated by the customer. This is very different information from information on customer satisfaction and/or dissatisfaction. Customer inspections/tests, field problem reports, and warranty returns are typical of customer information related to conformance to requirements.

Information on characteristics of processes, products, and their trends can be derived from analysis of product and process data obtained from the measurement process. This may also include information from aggregation and analysis of both internal operational data and feedback from customers.

Information on suppliers is information that can be developed from analysis of supplier performance data. It may include information on both excellent and poor performing suppliers. Since purchased material is often a significant percentage of total cost of goods sold, it makes business sense to invest appropriately in assuring excellent performance by suppliers (for example, zero defects or 100 percent on-time delivery).

HARDWARE AND PROCESSED MATERIALS

Information related to conformance to customer requirements may include such items as the most numerous/significant nonconformities reported by the customer, costs of customer returns, and significant design changes resulting from customer feedback. Information on characteristics of processes, products, and their trends may include process capabilities of manufacturing processes, types of significant assembly defects, order entry error rates and statistical process control data. It may also include such items as line balance information, cell cycle times, and other information needed to improve scheduling and cycle time.

SERVICES

Information related to conformance to customer requirements may include such items as significant nonconformities to customer requirements by customer-contact employees and/or service deliverers. The information may also include causes of late service performance, most significant reasons for service outages, opportunities to reduce unavailability of service due to over-capacity scheduling, inadequate documentation, billing, and other accounting errors.

Information on characteristics of processes, product, and their trends may include significant causes of process backlogs, ability of key service processes to deliver required services when requested by the customer, time needed to respond to service requests, satisfaction with delivered training, acceptability of consulting service, late delivery of service, and late and/or over-budget development projects.

SOFTWARE

Information related to conformance to customer requirements may include such items as the most numerous/significant nonconformities reported by the customer, the cost to correct a nonconformity, and issues related to installation and start-up.

Information on characteristics of processes, product, and their trends may include rate of decline of bugs found, on-time release, acceptability of design reviews, and controlling change.

 **DEFINITIONS**

Characteristic (2.5.1)—distinguishing feature

NOTE   There are various classes of characteristic, such as:

-physical, e.g. mechanical, electrical, chemical or biological characteristics;

-sensory, e.g. related to smell, touch, taste, sight, hearing;

-behavioural, e.g. courtesy, honesty, veracity;

-temporal, e.g. punctuality, reliability, availability;

-ergonomic, e.g. linguistic or physiological characteristic, or related to human safety;

-functional, e.g. range of a plane.

Customer (2.3.5)—organization or person that receives a product

EXAMPLES   Consumer, client, end-user, retailer, beneficiary and purchaser.

NOTE A supplier can be internal or external to the customer's organization.

Customer dissatisfaction (2.1.5)—customer's opinion of the degree to which a transaction has failed to meet the customer's needs and expectations

NOTE 1   A transaction is time and event specific and based on mutual needs and expectations and the communication of these between all parties concerned.

NOTE 2   Customer complaints are a common indicator of customer dissatisfaction with a transaction, but their absence does not necessarily imply customer satisfaction.

Customer satisfaction (2.1.6)—customer's opinion of the degree to which a transaction has met the customer's needs and expectations

NOTE   A transaction is time and event specific and based on mutual needs and expectations and the communication of these between all parties concerned.

Effectiveness (2.2.13)—measure of the extent to which planned activities are realized and planned results achieved

Management system (2.2.2)—system to establish policy and objectives and to achieve those objectives

NOTE   A management system of an organization may include different management systems, such as a quality

Process (2.4.1)—system of activities which uses resources to transform inputs into outputs

NOTE 1   Inputs to a process are typically outputs of other processes.

NOTE 2   Processes in an organization typically are planned and carried out under controlled conditions to add value.

NOTE 3   A process where the conformity of the resulting product cannot be readily or economically verified is frequently referred to as a "special process".

Measurement (2.10.1)—set of operations having the object of determining the value of a quantity

Measurement process (2.10.2)—set of interrelated resources, activities, and influences related to a measurement

NOTE 1   The resources concerned include measuring equipment, and measurement procedures and operators.

NOTE 2   Influences are all factors caused by the environment or procedures which may or may not be controlled or controllable and which add to the variability or the bias of the process.

Product (2.4.2)—result of a process

NOTE   There are four agreed generic product categories:

-hardware (e.g. engine mechanical part)

-software (e.g. computer program)

-services (e.g. transport)

-processed materials (e.g. lubricant)

Hardware and processed materials are generally tangible products, while software or services are generally intangible.

Most products comprise elements belonging to different generic product categories. Whether the product is then called hardware, processed material, software or service depends on the dominant element.

EXAMPLES The offered product "car" consists of hardware (e.g. the tyres), processed materials (e.g. fuel, cooling liquid), software (e.g. engine control software, the driver's manual), and service (e.g. the payment facilities or the guaranty).

Quality characteristic (2.5.2)—inherent characteristic of a product process or system derived from a requirement

NOTE   A characteristic assigned to a product, process or system (e.g. the price of a product) is not a quality characteristic of that product, process or system.

Requirement (2.1.2)—need or expectation that is stated, customarily implied or obligatory

NOTE 1   A qualifier may be used to denote a specific type of requirement, e.g. product requirement, quality system requirement, customer requirement.
NOTE 2   A specified requirement is one which is stated, for example, in a document.
NOTE 3   Requirements may be generated by different interested parties.

Source: BSR/ISO/ASQ Q9000-2000.

TYPICAL AUDIT ITEMS FOR COMPLIANCE

Items representing a difference from ISO 9001:1994 have a Δ at the end.

- Has the organization determined the appropriate data to be collected?
- Does the organization analyze the appropriate data to determine the suitability and effectiveness of the quality management system? Δ
- Does the organization analyze appropriate data to identify improvements that can be made? Δ
- Does the organization analyze appropriate data to provide information on customer satisfaction and/or dissatisfaction? Δ
- Does the organization analyze appropriate data to provide information on conformance to customer requirements? Δ
- Does the organization analyze appropriate data to provide information on characteristics of processes, product, and their trends? Δ
- Does the organization analyze appropriate data to provide information on suppliers? Δ

CHAPTER
12

Improvement

> ### 8.5.1 Planning for continual improvement
>
> The organization shall plan and manage the processes necessary for the continual improvement of the quality management system.
>
> The organization shall facilitate the continual improvement of the quality management system through the use of the quality policy, objectives, audit results, analysis of data, corrective and preventive action and management review.

Source: BSR/ISO/ASQ Q9001-2000.

Recall that clause 5.4.2 on quality planning (covered in Chapter 3) states that overall ". . . quality planning shall include: . . . continual improvement of the quality management system." This clause requires that the organization plan the processes related to this type of improvement. It is important to remember that the clear emphasis is on improving the quality management system.

Corrective and preventive action must be taken and are a key dimension of the continual improvement activities. They are further explained in clause 8.5.2 and clause 8.5.3.

 Procedures for corrective and preventive actions were required in ISO 9001:1994 and were intended to cause improvements in the quality management system. Clause 8.5.1 of ISO/DIS 9001:2000 goes on to list additional elements the organization must include to facilitate its planned improvement activities.

The quality policy must include continual improvement as an objective. Clause 5.3b requires that the policy include ". . . commitment to . . . continual improvement." Objectives must be used as an element of continual improvement. The setting of objectives consistent with continual improvement is required in clause 5.4.1 and is also discussed in Chapter 3.

Audit results form a key input in determining opportunities for continual improvement.

As discussed in Chapter 11, analysis of data must be performed to provide information to identify opportunities for improvement. Management review required by clause 5.6 provides a mechanism to ensure that top management reviews the status of corrective and preventive actions and determines actions related to improvement of the quality management system and its processes.

SERVICES, HARDWARE, PROCESSED MATERIALS, AND SOFTWARE

The practices required to comply with the general management clauses are essentially identical regardless of the category of product.

 DEFINITIONS

Organization (2.3.1)—group of people and facilities with an orderly arrangement of responsibilities, authorities and relationships

EXAMPLES   Company, corporation, firm, enterprise, institution, charity, sole trader, association, or parts or combination thereof.

NOTE 1   An organization can be incorporated, public or private.

NOTE 2   This definition is valid for the purposes of quality management systems standards. The term "organization" is defined differently in ISO/IEC Guide 2.

Process (2.4.1)—system of activities which uses resources to transform inputs into outputs

NOTE 1   Inputs to a process are typically outputs of other processes.

NOTE 2   Processes in an organization typically are planned and carried out under controlled conditions to add value.

NOTE 3   A process where the conformity of the resulting product cannot be readily or economically verified is frequently referred to as a "special process".

Quality management system (2.2.3)—system to establish a quality policy and quality objectives and to achieve those objectives

Quality objective (2.2.5)—something sought, or aimed for, related to quality

NOTE 1   Quality objectives should be based on the organization's quality policy

NOTE 2   Quality objectives are specified at different levels in the organization. At an operational level, quality objectives should be quantitative.

NOTE 3   Different terms are sometimes used for quality objectives, such as quality targets, quality aims or quality goals.

Quality policy (2.2.4)—overall intentions and directions of an organization related to quality as formally expressed by top management

NOTE 1   The quality policy should be consistent with the overall policy and provide a framework for the setting of quality objectives

NOTE 2   Quality management principles of this international standard may form a basis for the establishment of quality

Source: BSR/ISO/ASQ Q9000-2000.

 # TYPICAL AUDIT ITEMS FOR COMPLIANCE

Items representing a difference from ISO 9001:1994 have a Δ at the end.

- Does the organization plan and manage processes necessary for continual improvement of the quality management system? Δ

- Does the organization use quality policy, quality objectives, and analysis of data to facilitate continual improvement of the quality management system? Δ

- Does the organization use audit results, corrective action, and preventive action to facilitate continual improvement of the quality management system?

8.5.2 Corrective action

The organization shall take corrective action to eliminate the cause of nonconformities in order to prevent recurrence. Corrective action shall be appropriate to the impact of the problems encountered.

The documented procedure for corrective action shall define requirements for:

a) identifying nonconformities (including customer complaints);

b) determining the causes of nonconformity;

c) evaluating the need for actions to ensure that nonconformities do not recur;

d) determining and implementing the corrective action needed;

e) recording results of action taken;

f) reviewing of corrective action taken.

Source: BSR/ISO/ASQ Q9001-2000.

The corrective action concept has been a part of ISO 9001 from the beginning. It involves taking action to eliminate the causes of nonconformities.

Nonconformities must be identified in some manner so that the system can deal with them. This does not relate to the physical identification of nonconforming material covered in clause 8.3. Requirements for customer communications in clause 7.2.3 state that arrangements must be made with customers relating to complaints. Clause 8.5.2 requires that identification of nonconformities include these customer complaints. ISO 9001:1994 in clause 4.14.2 has a similar requirement for "the effective handling of customer complaints and reports of nonconformities." The words effective handling do not appear in ISO/DIS 9001:2000 since it is fundamental that all parts of the quality management system must be effective.

The process for determining the causes of nonconformities and complaints must be specified in the procedure. Organizations should focus the process on determining root causes. There must be a process to evaluate the need for actions to ensure that nonconformities do not recur. In some cases, action may neither be required nor appropriate. If the nonconformity is minor and an isolated condition, the risks or cost associated with taking corrective action may not be justified. Without this determination, resources may be diverted from identification and correction of the more important customer complaints and nonconformities. It is fundamental that the corrective actions taken be appropriate to the impact of the problem.

Nonconformities need to be evaluated, and the root causes of their occurrence need to be determined. Evaluations of the nonconformities should determine what action to take to correct the nonconformity and what action to take to eliminate the root cause of the nonconformity.

Once the action has been determined to correct the cause of the nonconformity, it needs to be implemented. The corrective action process must also provide for recording the results of the corrective actions taken. In ISO 9001:1994, clause 4.14.2d required "application of controls to ensure that corrective action is taken and that it is effective." In many organizations, a sign-off by someone who reviews the action taken and judges the effectiveness has been used to meet this requirement. The new standard is a bit more prescriptive in that the actual results of the corrective action must be recorded.

If actual results are recorded, the review for effectiveness can be conducted in a more objective manner. Review is required to ensure that the corrective actions have been implemented and are effective in preventing the problem from recurring.

SERVICES, HARDWARE, PROCESSED MATERIALS, AND SOFTWARE

The practices required to comply with the general management clauses are essentially identical regardless of the category of product.

 DEFINITIONS

Corrective action (2.6.5)—action taken to eliminate the cause of a detected nonconformity or other undesirable situation

NOTE 1   Corrective action is taken to prevent recurrence whereas preventive action is taken to prevent occurrence.
NOTE 2   There is a distinction between correction and corrective action.

Customer (2.3.5)—organization or person that receives a product

EXAMPLES   Consumer, client, end-user, retailer, beneficiary and purchaser.
NOTE   A supplier can be internal or external to the customer's organization.

Nonconformity (2.6.2)—nonfulfilment of a requirement

Requirement (2.1.2)—need or expectation that is stated, customarily implied or obligatory

NOTE 1   A qualifier may be used to denote a specific type of requirement, e.g. product requirement, quality system requirement, customer requirement.
NOTE 2   A specified requirement is one which is stated, for example, in a document.
NOTE 3   Requirements may be generated by different interested parties.

Review (2.8.6)—activity undertaken to ensure suitability, adequacy, effectiveness and efficiency of the subject matter to achieve established objectives

EXAMPLE   Management review, design and development review, review of customer requirements and nonconformity review.

Source: BSR/ISO/ASQ Q9000-2000.

CONSIDERATIONS FOR DOCUMENTATION

Clause 8.5.2 specifically requires a documented procedure for corrective action, and the procedure must provide for specific listed activities. This clause requires recording of the results of corrective action. There is no specific reference to clause 5.5.7 for control of the records generated. Organizations should consider maintaining quality records of corrective actions required, root causes found, actions taken, results of the actions, and review of the results to ensure the action was effective.

 TYPICAL AUDIT ITEMS FOR COMPLIANCE

Items representing a difference from ISO 9001:1994 have a Δ at the end.

* Does the organization take corrective action to eliminate causes of nonconformities?

* Is corrective action taken appropriate to the impact of the problems encountered?

* Do corrective action procedures provide for identifying nonconformities, determining causes, evaluating need for actions to prevent recurrence, determining the corrective action needed, and implementation of the needed corrective action?

* Do procedures for corrective action provide for recording the results of corrective actions taken? Δ

* Do the documented procedures for preventive action provide for reviewing the corrective action taken?

8.5.3 Preventive action

The organization shall identify preventive action to eliminate the causes of potential nonconformities to prevent occurrence. Preventive actions taken shall be appropriate to the impact of the potential problems.

The documented procedure for preventive action shall define requirements for:

a) identifying potential nonconformities and their causes;

b) determining and ensuring the implementation of preventive action needed;

c) recording results of action taken;

d) reviewing of preventive action taken.

Source: BSR/ISO/ASQ Q9001-2000.

The concept of preventive action was added to ISO 9001 in the 1994 revision, and the preventive action requirements in ISO/DIS 9001:2000 are not intended to be different from the 1994 version. Many organizations do not separate the concepts and use the same process for both corrective action and preventive action. Actually the concepts are somewhat different, and the techniques are different for each. While corrective action involves the solving of known problems, preventive action is intended to address finding potential causes of possible problems. In preventive action the organization is required to identify preventive action to eliminate the "cause of potential nonconformities".

It is not intended that the organization identify every possible nonconformity that could be envisioned, but there must be a defined method to identify those for which the organization chooses to take preventive action. Organizations have the freedom to define this in a manner that best suits their business situation. There are a number of ways to identify potential problems and to assess their potential impact. Some examples include the following:

- When nonconformities are identified in one part of the organization and causes are addressed by the corrective action system, some organizations look for similar situations in other areas. For example, if action is taken to correct the cause of a nonconformity for one product line, it may be desirable to determine if similar nonconformities are likely for other lines. If so, preventive action may be appropriate for the other lines.

- Risk analysis or failure modes and effects analysis may be used to define potential problems and to assess their potential impacts.

- Analysis of data on process performance may identify process parameters that have a high probability of creating nonconformities.

- Management review may be used as a vehicle for discussing and evaluating areas for preventive actions.

The documented procedure must also provide for determining and ensuring the implementation of preventive actions to eliminate the potential causes identified.

As with corrective action, ISO 9001:2000 requires that the results of the preventive actions taken be recorded. In many organizations, a sign-off by someone who reviews the action taken and judges the effectiveness has been used to meet this requirement. The new standard is a bit more prescriptive in that the actual results of the corrective action must be recorded. If actual results are recorded, the review for effectiveness can be conducted in a more objective manner. This implies that there will be some information or data recorded to verify that the potential nonconformity has not occurred over some reasonable time period. Review is required to ensure that the preventive actions have been implemented and are effective in preventing the potential problem from occurring.

SERVICES, HARDWARE, PROCESSED MATERIALS, AND SOFTWARE

The practices required to comply with the general management clauses are essentially identical regardless of the category of product.

 DEFINITIONS

Nonconformity (2.6.2)—nonfulfilment of a requirement

Preventive action (2.6.4)—action taken to eliminate the cause of a potential nonconformity or other potentially undesirable situation

NOTE   Preventive action is taken to prevent occurrence whereas corrective action is taken to prevent recurrence.

Requirement (2.1.2)—need or expectation that is stated, customarily implied or obligatory

NOTE 1   A qualifier may be used to denote a specific type of requirement, e.g. product requirement, quality system requirement, customer requirement.
NOTE 2   A specified requirement is one which is stated, for example, in a document.
NOTE 3   Requirements may be generated by different interested parties.

Review (2.8.6)—activity undertaken to ensure suitability, adequacy, effectiveness and efficiency of the subject matter to achieve established objectives

EXAMPLE   Management review, design and development review, review of customer requirements and nonconformity review.

Source: BSR/ISO/ASQ Q9000-2000.

 CONSIDERATIONS FOR DOCUMENTATION

As with corrective action, the organization is required to have a documented procedure to define specific activities. Clause 8.5.3 requires records of preventive action results with no specific reference to clause 5.5.7 for control of the records generated. Organizations should consider maintaining quality records of preventive action projects undertaken, potential root causes found, actions taken, results of the actions, and review of the results to ensure the action was effective.

 TYPICAL AUDIT ITEMS FOR COMPLIANCE

Items representing a difference from ISO 9001:1994 have a Δ at the end.

- Does the organization identify preventive actions needed to eliminate the potential causes of possible nonconformities?
- Is preventive action taken appropriate to the impact of potential problems?
- Do the documented procedures for preventive action provide for identifying potential nonconformities and their probable causes?
- Do the documented procedures for preventive action provide for determining the need for preventive action and implementation of the preventive action needed?
- Do the documented procedures for preventive action provide for recording the results of the preventive actions taken? Δ
- Do the documented procedures for preventive action provide for reviewing the preventive action taken?

Annex

Note: This annex is Annex B of BSR/ISO/ASQ Q9001-2000.

ANNEX B

(informative)

Correspondence between ISO/DIS 9001:2000 and ISO 9001:1994

Table B.1   Correspondence between ISO 9001:1994
and ISO/DIS 9001:2000

ISO 9001:1994	ISO/DIS 9001:2000
1 Scope	1
2 Normative reference	2
3 Definitions	3
4.1 Management responsibility	
4.1.1 Quality policy	5.1 + 5.3 + 5.4.1
4.1.2 Organization	5.5.2
4.1.2.1 Responsibility and authority	5.5.2 + 6.2.1
4.1.2.2 Resources	5.1 + 6.1 + 6.3
4.1.2.3 Management representative	5.5.3
4.1.3 Management review	5.6
4.2 Quality system	
4.2.1 General	4.× + 5.1 + 5.4.1 + 5.5.5
4.2.2 Quality system procedures	4.2
4.2.3 Quality planning	5.4.2 + 7.1
4.3 Contract review	7.2.2
4.4 Design control	7.3
4.5 Document and data control	5.5.6
4.6 Purchasing	7.4
4.7 Control of customer-supplied product	7.5.3
4.8 Product identification and traceability	7.5.2

(Continued)

Table B.1   Continued.

ISO 9001:1994	ISO/DIS 9001:2000
4.9 Process control	7.1 + 7.5.1 + 7.5.5
4.10 Inspection and testing	7.1 + 7.5.1 + 8.1 + 8.2.4
4.11 Control of inspection, measuring and test equipment	7.6
4.12 Inspection and test status	7.5.1
4.13 Control of nonconforming product	8.3
4.14 Corrective and preventive action	8.4 + 8.5.2 + 8.5.3
4.15 Handling, storage, packaging, preservation and delivery	7.1 + 7.5.4
4.16 Control of quality records	5.5.7
4.17 Internal quality audits	8.2.2
4.18 Training	6.2.2
4.19 Servicing	7.1 + 7.5.1
4.20 Statistical techniques	8.1 + 8.2.3 + 8.2.4 + 8.4

Source: BSR/ISO/ASQ Q9001-2000.

Table B.2   Correspondence between ISO/DIS 9001:2000
               and ISO 9001:1994

ISO/DIS 9001:2000	ISO 9001:1994
1 Scope	1
1.1 General	
1.2 Permissible exclusions	
2 Normative references	2
3 Terms and definitions	3
4 Quality management system	
4.1 General requirements	4.2.1

(Continued)

Table B.2   Continued.

ISO/DIS 9001:2000	ISO 9001:1994
4.2 General documentation requirements	4.2.2
5 Management responsibility	
5.1 Management commitment	4.1 + 4.1.2.2 + 4.2.1
5.2 Customer focus	
5.3 Quality policy	4.1.1
5.4 Planning	
5.4.1 Quality objectives	4.1.1 + 4.2.1
5.4.2 Quality planning	4.2.3
5.5 Administration	
5.5.1 General	
5.5.2 Responsibility and authority	4.1.2 + 4.1.2.1
5.5.3 Management representative	4.1.2.3
5.5.4 Internal communication	
5.5.5 Quality Manual	4.2.1
5.5.6 Control of documents	4.5
5.5.7 Control of quality records	4.16
5.6 Management review	4.1.3
5.6.1 Review input	4.1.3
5.6.2 Review output	4.1.3
6 Resource management	4.1.2.2
6.1 Provision of resources	4.1.2.2
6.2 Human resources	
6.2.1 Assignment of personnel	4.1.2.1

(Continued)

Table B.2   Continued.

ISO/DIS 9001:2000	ISO 9001:1994
6.2.2 Training, awareness and competency	4.18
6.3 Facilities	4.9
6.4 Work environment	4.9
7 Product realization	
7.1 Planning of realization processes	4.2.3 + 4.9 + 4.10 + 4.15 + 4.19
7.2 Customer-related processes	
7.2.1 Identification of customer requirements	
7.2.2 Review of product requirements	4.3
7.2.3 Customer communication	
7.3 Design and/or development	4.4
7.3.1 Design and/or development planning	4.4.2 + 4.4.3
7.3.2 Design and/or development inputs	4.4.4
7.3.3 Design and/or development outputs	4.4.5
7.3.4 Design and/or development review	4.4.6
7.3.5 Design and/or development verification	4.4.7
7.3.6 Design and/or development validation	4.4.8
7.3.7 Control of design and/or development changes	4.4.9
7.4 Purchasing	
7.4.1 Purchasing control	4.6
7.4.2 Purchasing information	4.6
7.4.3 Verification of purchased products	4.6

(Continued)

Table B.2   Continued.

ISO/DIS 9001:2000	ISO 9001:1994
7.5 Production and service operations	
7.5.1 Operations control	4.9 + 4.10 + 4.12 + 4.19
7.5.2 Identification and traceability	4.8
7.5.3 Customer property	4.7
7.5.4 Preservation of product	4.15
7.5.5 Validation of processes	4.9
7.6 Control of measuring and monitoring devices	4.11
8 Measurement, analysis and improvement	
8.1 Planning	4.10 + 4.20
8.2 Measurement and monitoring	
8.2.1 Customer satisfaction	
8.2.2 Internal audit	4.17
8.2.3 Measurement and monitoring of processes	4.20
8.2.4 Measurement and monitoring of product	4.10 + 4.20
8.3 Control of nonconformity	4.13
8.4 Analysis of data	4.14 + 4.20
8.5 Improvement	
8.5.1 Planning for continual improvement	4.1.3 + 4.9
8.5.2 Corrective action	4.14
8.5.3 Preventive action	4.14

Source: BSR/ISO/ASQ Q9001-2000.

Index